MACMILLAN MASTER GUIDES

TELEPEN

D0243875

GENERAL EDITOR: JAMES GIB

Published

60960

JANE AUSTEN	*Emma* Norman Page
	Persuasion Judy Simons
	Sense and Sensibility Judy Simons
	Pride and Prejudice Raymond Wilson
	Mansfield Park Richard Wirdnam
SAMUEL BECKETT	*Waiting for Godot* Jennifer Birkett
WILLIAM BLAKE	*Songs of Innocence* and *Songs of Experience* Alan Tomlinson
ROBERT BOLT	*A Man for All Seasons* Leonard Smith
CHARLOTTE BRONTË	*Jane Eyre* Robert Miles
EMILY BRONTË	*Wuthering Heights* Hilda D. Spear
GEOFFREY CHAUCER	*The Miller's Tale* Michael Alexander
	The Pardoner's Tale Geoffrey Lester
	The Wife of Bath's Tale Nicholas Marsh
	The Knight's Tale Anne Samson
	The Prologue to the Canterbury Tales Nigel Thomas and Richard Swan
JOSEPH CONRAD	*The Secret Agent* Andrew Mayne
CHARLES DICKENS	*Bleak House* Dennis Butts
	Great Expectations Dennis Butts
	Hard Times Norman Page
GEORGE ELIOT	*Middlemarch* Graham Handley
	Silas Marner Graham Handley
	The Mill on the Floss Helen Wheeler
T. S. ELIOT	*Murder in the Cathedral* Paul Lapworth
	Selected Poems Andrew Swarbrick
HENRY FIELDING	*Joseph Andrews* Trevor Johnson
E. M. FORSTER	*Howards End* Ian Milligan
	A Passage to India Hilda D. Spear
WILLIAM GOLDING	*The Spire* Rosemary Sumner
	Lord of the Flies Raymond Wilson
OLIVER GOLDSMITH	*She Stoops to Conquer* Paul Ranger
THOMAS HARDY	*The Mayor of Casterbridge* Ray Evans
	Tess of the d'Urbervilles James Gibson
	Far from the Madding Crowd Colin Temblett-Wood
GERARD MANLEY HOPKINS	*Selected Poems* R. J. C. Watt
JOHN KEATS	*Selected Poems* John Garrett
BEN JONSON	*Volpone* Michael Stout
PHILIP LARKIN	*The Whitsun Weddings* and *The Less Deceived* Andrew Swarbrick
D. H. LAWRENCE	*Sons and Lovers* R. P. Draper
HARPER LEE	*To Kill a Mockingbird* Jean Armstrong
LAURIE LEE	*Cider with Rosie* Brian Tarbitt

MACMILLAN MASTER GUIDES

CHRISTOPHER MARLOWE	*Doctor Faustus* David A. Male
THE METAPHYSICAL POETS	Joan van Emden
THOMAS MIDDLETON and WILLIAM ROWLEY	*The Changeling* Tony Bromham
ARTHUR MILLER	*The Crucible* Leonard Smith *Death of a Salesman* Peter Spalding
GEORGE ORWELL	*Animal Farm* Jean Armstrong
WILLIAM SHAKESPEARE	*Richard II* Charles Barber *Hamlet* Jean Brooks *Othello* Tony Bromham *King Lear* Francis Casey *Henry V* Peter Davison *The Winter's Tale* Diana Devlin *Julius Caesar* David Elloway *Macbeth* David Elloway *The Merchant of Venice* A. M. Kinghorn *Measure for Measure* Mark Lilly *Henry IV Part I* Helen Morris *A Midsummer Night's Dream* Kenneth Pickering *Romeo and Juliet* Helen Morris *The Tempest* Kenneth Pickering *Coriolanus* Gordon Williams *Antony and Cleopatra* Martin Wine
GEORGE BERNARD SHAW	*St Joan* Leonée Ormond
RICHARD SHERIDAN	*The School for Scandal* Paul Ranger *The Rivals* Jeremy Rowe
ALFRED TENNYSON	*In Memoriam* Richard Gill
ANTHONY TROLLOPE	*Barchester Towers* K. M. Newton
JOHN WEBSTER	*The White Devil* and *The Duchess of Malfi* David A. Male
VIRGINIA WOOLF	*To the Lighthouse* John Mepham *Mrs Dalloway* Julian Pattison
WILLIAM WORDSWORTH	*The Prelude Books I and II* Helen Wheeler

Forthcoming

JOHN BUNYAN	*The Pilgrim's Progress* Beatrice Batson
RUDYARD KIPLING	*Kim* Leonée Ormond
JOHN MILTON	*Comus* Tom Healy
WILLIAM SHAKESPEARE	*As You Like It* Kiernan Ryan
W. B. YEATS	*Selected Poems* Stan Smith

MACMILLAN MASTER GUIDES

THE PRELUDE

BOOKS I AND II

BY WILLIAM WORDSWORTH

HELEN WHEELER

MACMILLAN
EDUCATION

First edition 1988

Published by
MACMILLAN EDUCATION LTD
Houndmills, Basingstoke, Hampshire RG21 2XS
and London
Companies and representatives
throughout the world

Typeset by TecSet Ltd, Wallington, Surrey
Printed in Hong Kong

British Library Cataloguing in Publication Data
Wheeler, Helen
The prelude books I and II by William
Wordsworth.—(Macmillan master guides).
1. Wordsworth, William, *1770–1850*.
Prelude, The. Book 1 & 2
I. Title II. Wordsworth, William,
1770–1850. Prelude
821'.7   PR5864
ISBN 0–333–44279–2 Pbk
ISBN 0–333–44280–6 Pbk export

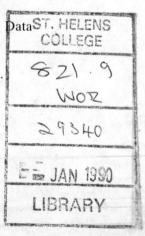

CONTENTS

GENERAL EDITOR'S PREFACE

The aim of the Macmillan Master Guides is to help you to appreciate
the book you are studying by providing information about it and by
suggesting ways of reading and thinking about it which will lead to a
fuller understanding. The section on the writer's life and background
has been designed to illustrate those aspects of the writer's life which
have influenced the work, and to place it in its personal and literary
context. The summaries and critical commentary are of special
importance in that each brief summary of the action is followed by an
examination of the significant critical points. The space which might
have been given to repetitive explanatory notes has been devoted to a
detailed analysis of the kind of passage which might confront you in
an examination. Literary criticism is concerned with both the broader
aspects of the work being studied and with its detail. The ideas which
meet us in reading a great work of literature, and their relevance to us
today, are an essential part of our study, and our Guides look at the
thought of their subject in some detail. But just as essential is the
craft with which the writer has constructed his work of art, and this
may be considered under several technical headings — character-
isation, language, style and stagecraft, for example.

The authors of these Guides are all teachers and writers of wide
experience, and they have chosen to write about books they admire
and know well in the belief that they can communicate their
admiration to you. But you yourself must read and know intimately
the book you are studying. No one can do that for you. You should
see this book as a lamp-post. Use it to shed light, not to lean against.
If you know your text and know what it is saying about life, and how
it says it, then you will enjoy it, and there is no better way of passing
an examination in literature.

JAMES GIBSON

ACKNOWLEDGEMENTS

Quotations from the poem are taken from the *Norton Critical Edition: The Prelude*, edited by Jonathan Wordsworth, M. H. Abrams and Stephen Gill.

Cover illustration: *View of Tarn Crag from Langdale Pikes*. Photograph reproduced by courtesy of Amanda Maxwell.

1 WILLIAM WORDSWORTH: LIFE AND BACKGROUND

1.1 WORDSWORTH'S LIFE IN RELATION TO *THE PRELUDE*

If we were to judge solely from the account in *The Prelude*, Wordsworth's boyhood appears to be one of the most glorious freedom. From his earliest years, he roamed the country round, valley and mountain, winter and summer, by day and night. He skated, galloped, went bird's-nesting and boating, sometimes alone but often with a lively group of friends: 'We were a noisy crew', he says happily. On summer evenings the market square at Hawkshead resounded to their noise long after the villagers had gone to bed, and in the winter there were cheerful games of cards, puzzles and word-games. All these energetic boyhood pleasures, both solitary and convivial, took place in a countryside as magnificently beautiful as it is various. Meanwhile no one, even at school, ever seemed to have told young Wordsworth or his friends to be home by a certain hour, or indeed to worry if they were out all night, or to warn them of the dangers of rock-climbing or to tell them to make less noise: the freedom of space and countryside was mirrored by a psychological freedom from controls. Amid this 'delightful round' the boy became increasingly aware of a strong, protective monitory power in every aspect of the natural world around him, to which he responded with physical and emotional energy and joy.

So it is with surprise that we discover how sad were many of the factual circumstances of William's young life. His mother died when he was eight years old and his dear sister Dorothy was sent away to relations for a nine-year-long 'separation desolate'. Five years later his father also died, leaving his affairs in such disorder that for a very long time Wordsworth would be plagued by money troubles and suffer the small but bitter indignities, in school holidays, of being a dependent poor relation.

William was born in 1770 in Cockermouth where his parents were people of standing. His mother Ann came from Penrith and married John Wordsworth in 1766 when she was just eighteen. For the whole of her brief married life of twelve years she lived in the fine, spacious house (still standing today) that her husband occupied as man of business to the local magnate, Sir James Lowther. In this house she bore five children. The eldest was Richard, who was to become a cautious lawyer, advising his brothers and sister financially; then came William in April 1770 and the only daughter, Dorothy, on Christmas Day, 1771. John, a singularly gentle, shy boy to whom William became devoted, was next: he later entered the Merchant Navy. Finally, in 1774 came Christopher, scholarly and ambitious, who eventually became Master of Trinity College, Cambridge.

The garden of the Cockermouth house ran down to the River Derwent and it was the murmur of this river which was Wordsworth's earliest conscious memory, supplying the child with a symbol of time and change and of life itself. He remembered, too, running naked in fields of yellow ragwort, higher than himself at the age of five. His mother seems to have been serenely unworried by possibilities of danger but to have given her children the strongest sense of protective love, providing 'in tenderness and love / A centre to the circle which they make' (V.251–2). Wordsworth saw the relationship between mother and child as a pattern of the relationship between the child and the universe itself (II.232–65) and his conception of Nature as 'nurse . . . guide . . . guardian of my heart' clearly derives from his infant relationship with his mother.

He knew his father, John, less well, though his love of literature meant the boy was encouraged to learn great portions of Shakespeare and Milton by heart and was allowed to revel in his father's library of novels and romances. Immersion in literature of this kind he always defended as an essential part of education, since books like *Robinson Crusoe*, *Tom Jones* and *The Arabian Nights* prepared him for strange and horrific events in real life. John Wordsworth was totally involved in the job of managing the economic and political interests of Lowther, and his position as this unpopular man's representative carried many consequences. It distanced him from the townsfolk: Dorothy said how it grieved her after his death to find they had no real friends in Cockermouth. It was his devotion to his work that brought about his early death after being benighted in December among the hills – a devotion made ironic by the discovery after his death that Lowther owed him thousands of pounds which he refused to pay (the debt was only settled by Lowther's heir in 1802). So the unfortunate little Wordsworths suddenly found themselves orphaned, turned out of their beautiful home, and nearly penniless.

By this time William was a boarder at Hawkshead Grammar School, where all the brothers were educated. This market town lies at the northern end of a valley almost totally filled by the Esthwaite: at the southern end a steep road leads down to Lake Windermere and, from the age of ten until eighteen, these two valleys were the mould of Wordsworth's imaginative life. The school itself had a very high academic reputation and attracted pupils from as far as Edinburgh. About a hundred students were there at this time and many went on to Cambridge. Everything combined to make Wordsworth's school life very happy: he made many friends; he lodged, as did about half the boys, not in the schoolhouse but half a mile away with a singularly tolerant and kindly landlady, Ann Tyson; he loved his classics and was taught mathematics so well that he found he had no need to work in his first year at Cambridge. Nor should we assume that the education given at Hawkshead was confined to a narrow classics/mathematics curriculum. The schoolmaster, William Taylor, was a remarkable man who seems to have passed on to his pupils his admiration for Newton and Bacon and the modern, experimental approach to knowledge, as well as his enthusiasm for recent poetry like that of Thomas Chatterton and Robert Burns which Wordsworth could not otherwise have encountered. The first two books of *The Prelude* vividly convey the freedom of the life they led outside the classroom, though some of the schoolday episodes appear later in the poem (see Section 2.1). Wordsworth found himself fascinated by solitary figures such as shepherds and vagrants. He made friends with one of these, an old Scottish pedlar, whom he often accompanied on walks, hearing him recite from his great store of ballads and listening intently to his 'home-felt wisdom'.

Holidays were sometimes less happy: his father's brother Richard provided a congenial home at Whitehaven, but summers were spent at Penrith with his maternal grandparents and his unpleasant Uncle Kit. Of this narrowly conventional household both William and Dorothy retained miserable memories, the latter describing how the four children once wept together when realisation of their orphaned state had been borne in upon them particularly sharply by a servant's rudeness because of their poverty. William became so miserable that (according to his own recollections) when he came across some old foils in an attic, he contemplated suicide. Yet even here he found brilliant moments of joy: a reunion with Dorothy, though temporary, renewed for him the tenderness he had known from his mother, and he realised that now he had someone to share his passion for poetry and nature.

When he was eighteen, Wordsworth went to St John's College, Cambridge, and his life now passes beyond the bounds of the first two books of *The Prelude*, but it is necessary to know about his adult life as well in order to understand the compulsions that drove him to record his childhood and adolescence with such care. After Cambridge he still had no idea how he was to earn a living, though he was convinced of his vocation to be a poet. The conventional solution for a man of his qualifications was to become a clergyman, a prospect

Wordsworth viewed with horror, particularly as his more cautious relations all urged it strongly. Instead, like many other students, he decided that a stint abroad might solve his problems. He therefore went to France, where he found himself in a worsening revolution. His traumatic experiences here, his political education by the French revolutionary soldier, Michel Beaupuy, his ill-fated love affair with Annette Vallon, his extraordinary sojourn in the Paris of Robespierre, and his despair at the 'calamitous' state in which he found England upon his return, are described in Section 3.

In 1795 a small legacy from a friend started a new period in his life: it was not only that his frugal independence would leave him free to write poetry, but Dorothy could at last fulfil her life's ambition and come to keep house for him. First they tried Dorset, but then moved to Somerset to be near a new friend, Samuel Taylor Coleridge. A quite remarkable creative symbiosis seems to have taken place between Wordsworth and Coleridge, each inspiring the other to work they could not otherwise have achieved. The *Lyrical Ballads*, regarded by many critics as a manifesto of a new kind of poetry in England, was their joint effort in 1798. After a shared visit to Germany, where Wordsworth first began the writing of *The Prelude*, Coleridge accompanied William and Dorothy when they made their final remove in 1799 back to the Lake District of their childhood.

William's marriage to Mary Hutchinson in 1802 was a deeply happy one, as a recent fortunate discovery of their love letters revealed, but this did not mean a separation from Dorothy, who helped them care for the five children who were born. The old Lowther debt was paid at last, and in the domestic serenity of his home, living in the countryside which spoke so powerfully to him, Wordsworth's life became settled and secure – or so it seemed. By 1820 he was regarded as a major poet. He had a wealthy friend and patron in Sir George Beaumont, a useful salary from a civil service job as Stamp Distributor for Westmorland, and in 1843, not very willingly, he became Poet Laureate.

As often with Wordsworth, however, there is a darker, fugal element: the great partnership with Coleridge had petered out in disillusion and misunderstanding; gentle John Wordsworth, the favourite brother, was drowned when the vessel he captained sank off Weymouth in 1805; two children died young, leaving the sense of unutterable loss that such deaths always bring; Dora, always her father's favourite, also died after a brief marriage; Dorothy developed Alzheimer's disease in her late fifties, and the distressing change in her nature and the failure of her powers cast a shadow over the devoted family. Above all Wordsworth knew, though he continued writing, that the springing inspiration of his early years had gone, and only very rarely, as in his famous 1835 lament for so many of the poets he had once known, could he achieve lines like 'How fast has brother followed brother / From sunshine to the sunless land'.

Perhaps success and security do not really suit a poet. Of the remarkable cluster of poets who flourished between 1798 and 1824, called the Romantics, Wordsworth was the only one to survive into old age, John Keats and Percy Bysshe Shelley not even making thirty. When he was a young man, Wordsworth had been fiercely attacked for being radical and revolutionary: when he was old the young poet Robert Browning attacked him for betraying his ideals and joining forces with the Tory party and the Anglican church, ignoring the way his concern for the unfortunate and his own practical charity had never faltered. The mass of later poetry became a barrier to the contemporary appreciation of *The Prelude* when at last it was published on Wordsworth's death in 1850, especially as by then the mid-Victorian image of him was primarily that of a comforting antidote to the urban materialism of the mid-century. For the reader of *The Prelude*, it is essential to see the poet against the very different background of the turn of the century.

1.2 WORDSWORTH'S COUNTRY

Of all great English poets, Wordsworth is the one most naturally associated with a particular area: the counties of Cumberland and Westmorland, or as they came to be called, the Lake District. This is an area of about eighty square miles lying in the north-west corner of England, just south of the Scottish border and surrounded on three sides by the sea. Its mountains are not really high, the highest, Scafell Pike, being under 1000 metres, but their nearness to the sea and to less dramatic country to the east makes them appear very impressive. The majestic effect is heightened by very individual shapes and the way they sweep down, not to marshy valleys but to mirroring lakes. The fifteen main lakes radiate like spokes of a wheel, the centre being, roughly, Wordsworth's home at Grasmere. The ancient, weathered rocks, deep valleys and sudden, startling skylines provide an immensely varied scenery which had attracted visitors well before Wordsworth's influence was to make it, to his dismay, even more popular.

The famous William Gilpin (1724–1804), himself a native of Cumberland, devoted his energies to educating his contemporaries about the nature of the picturesque, teaching them to look in a landscape for the same 'sublime' and striking contrasts they would find in a painting by Salvator Rosa or Claude Lorrain. He particularly admired the Lakes and said approvingly: 'Beauty lying in the lap of Horror'. The imposition of these concepts upon the innocent landscape was accompanied by all sorts of efforts of entrepreneurs to stimulate the tourist's sense of the sublime: on Ullswater, musical instruments were played on the pleasure-boats to arouse the echoes and, for an extra fee, six brass cannon, swivel mounted, were fired off in turn to produce stunning echoes 'seven times repeated' from the peaks around. It is easy to imagine Wordsworth's indignation at this commercial exploitation of his countryside, and when he was an old man, he tried his hardest to keep out the railway, whose proliferation he blamed upon 'the thirst for gold'. He thought that the true lover of mountains could, as he and Dorothy and Coleridge did so often in the past, travel on foot. In 1844 he wrote an angry sonnet on the proposed new line, in which he identifies himself with his 'beloved retreats': 'Hear YE that whistle?', he asks them, and goes on: 'Mountains and Vales and Floods, I call on you / To share the passion of a just disdain'. Of course, the railway did come and brought in its wake even more visitors.

For some of these Wordsworth himself had become the magnet. Literally hundreds of summer visitors turned up each year, and fellow writers such as Southey, Coleridge and de Quincey all settled nearby. For both 'Tourists and Residents' Wordsworth wrote 'A Guide to the Lakes', which appeared in ever new editions and revisions from 1810 until 1864, and became an immensely popular book. Indeed, Matthew Arnold reported, perhaps as a joke, that a clerical visitor enquired if Wordsworth had ever written anything else. What this little book demonstrates is the way Wordsworth taught the nineteenth century that they must look around them with different eyes, not demanding the sublime and the picturesque and categorising landscapes in terms of ideal beauty, but surrendering to the thing itself so that they could learn the lessons which Nature would teach to 'the heart that watches and receives'.

For Wordsworth, his native country far surpassed the mountainous country of Wales, Scotland and even of Switzerland. He explains why: his mountains are of the best height, 'an elevation of 3,000 feet' to allow of 'compact and fleecy clouds settling upon or sweeping over their summits'. Equally he prefers his own lakes: 'they are more happily proportioned . . . more pellucid', whereas Swiss lakes are 'not pure to the eye, but of a heavy green hue' and therefore unable to produce 'those beautiful repetitions of surrounding objects in the bosom of the water, which are so frequently seen here: not to speak of the fine dazzling, trembling network, breezy motions and streaks and circles of intermingled smooth and rippled water which makes the surface of our lakes a field of endless variety'. Wordsworth's enthusiasm is instructive, for we notice that what specially matters to him is the animation of constant change and movement, the contrast between the turbulence of waterfalls and the stillness of lakes, the abrupt variation of weather, the continuously changing colours of vegetation with the succeeding months.

Many visitors then and now complain of the frequent rain in the Lake District. Wordsworth will have none of this. Instead he celebrates the consequent effect of 'every brook and torrent sonorous' and how the swift movements of clouds and mists 'give a visionary character to everything around them'. As always, the clouds in his perception assume their own individual life: 'such clouds, cleaving to their stations, or lifting up suddenly their glittering heads from behind rocky barriers, or hurrying out of sight with speed of the sharpest edge'. He makes them sound like Milton's angels, and in contrast he points to the 'cerulean vacancy' of the Italian sky, 'an unanimated and even a sad spectacle'.

2 THE PRELUDE

2.1 THE THREE VERSIONS OF THE POEM

There are three versions of *The Prelude*, each of which reached the definitive stage of a fair manuscript copy, quite apart from innumerable separate passages, draft copies and emendations. As a result many lines have alternative readings often of great interest. This brief note puts the three versions into context.

Wordsworth spent the winter of 1798–9 with his sister Dorothy at Goslar in Germany. The comparative isolation of their life there, short of money, with few books and without the companionship of Coleridge, seems to have directed Wordsworth's creative energies powerfully back to his early years; he began a poem about his childhood and boyhood. This was finished by December 1799, when he was back in England. It consists of just under a thousand lines and is divided into two parts, the second being roughly equivalent to the second part of the 1805 and 1850 versions. The first part, however, is considerably different from these. It plunges at once into Wordsworth's earliest childhood memories of playing beside the River Derwent, that is, it begins at what is line 269 of the 1850 version and contains eleven incidents from his childhood, some of which were of an extremely traumatic nature. The first of these occurred when he was five years old. On a journey he became separated from his father's servant who was looking after him. Suddenly he found himself at the site of an old gibbet where a murderer had hung in chains; hurrying away from this he encountered a solitary girl carrying a pitcher, struggling against the high wind near the summit of the hill. Then when he was nine, he had watched a drowned man being hauled out of Esthwaite Water. A third episode describes him as waiting to be taken home from school for the Christmas holidays when he was twelve. The desolate hillside from where he watched for the horses became imprinted on his mind when his father abruptly died a few days later. Wordsworth describes these events as 'spots of time' where understanding of the recollected past could bring 'profoundest knowledge' of the present. The 1799 version uses the general pattern of narrative/descriptive passages interspersed with meditations aroused by them, so that Wordsworth seems to be using the poem as an attempt to discover the truth about human nature and the nature of the visible world, his younger self acting as the evidence needed for this investigation. Over the years, the poem grows to encompass a much longer time span, but this basic pattern remains unchanged.

In 1804 Wordsworth resumed work on the poem and by May 1805 he had rewritten and extended it to thirteen books. He had prefixed the long opening passage (I.1–269), which explains why he had chosen the subject of his own life; he had moved the incidents described above from their chronological position to Books V and XII; and he had continued his story to include Cambridge, his experiences in revolutionary France and afterwards in London, and his final recovery of serenity with his return to the country of his upbringing.

Subsequently there were three reworkings of the 1805 text, new fair copies being made in 1816–19, 1832 and 1839, the last of these providing the basis for the 1850 edition. The major changes were the division of Book X into two, so that the final version is in fourteen books, and the wholesale removal of a sad little love story about two characters called Vaudracour and Julia, which he published separately in 1820. This tale is a heavily disguised version of the love affair with Annette Vallon in 1792, and its removal is perhaps representative of Wordsworth's increasing conformity to traditional points of view. Certainly other differences between the later and earlier versions have roused much critical argument as to which is the 'best' or the most truly representative of Wordsworth. The later version conforms more carefully with orthodox Christian interpretation, rather than finding nature as all-sufficient, and some stylistic changes can be seen as sacrificing spontaneity for greater formality. Yet in these first two books the voice of the young Wordsworth comes over clearly in spite of fifty years of revision.

The unprecedentedly long delay in publishing arose from Wordsworth's view of *The Prelude* as merely the 'least important' part of a much longer philosophical poem he planned to write, to be called *The Recluse*. To publish a poem with so much about himself would only be justified when he could follow the history of his own development with the philosophical system to which it led. Of this projected poem Wordsworth only achieved fragments. When he died in 1850, his greatest poem still did not have a title – it had been referred to over the years as *Poem to Coleridge*, *Poem on the Growth of a Poet's*

Mind, *Poem on My Own Life* or, simply, as in the 1805 manuscript, as *Poem – Title not yet fixed upon*. When William was dead it was his wife Mary who suggested the title of the poem: *The Prelude*.

2.2 BRIEF SUMMARY OF *THE PRELUDE*

Book I starts with Wordsworth's uneasy search for a suitable theme for an epic poem. In the midst of his uncertainty, the recollection of the delight and power which nature gave him in his boyhood makes him recognise that this is his proper theme: to rediscover and to identify the forces that shaped his own creative imagination. The poem is thus profoundly autobiographical, but it is not chronological or comprehensive, since Wordsworth only concerns himself with what is relevant to his development as a poet. Nor is historical accuracy of great importance: sometimes every detail known to us fits exactly with the episode described, but sometimes two or more experiences are drawn together. In Book I he recalls his earliest memory of playing beside the Derwent, setting bird-traps at night on the hills, bird's-nesting, rowing by moonlight in an illicitly borrowed boat on Ullswater, skating, nutting, fishing, flying kites and, in the winter, hearing the ice splitting in the lakes nearby while he and his friends play endless games in the comfortable warmth of their cottage. As will happen throughout the poem, the pattern is of narration interspersed with meditations in which Wordsworth tries to reconcile what he remembers with the psychological impact upon his growing awareness.

Book II carries this pattern further through his schooldays, with the rowdy games they all played in the market square at Hawkshead, boating on Windermere, and long excursions on horseback to Furness Abbey. He reflects upon the close relationship between a new-born baby and its mother, and sees this as the first source of its instinctive unity with the natural world; he immediately goes on to explore other and much later examples of this unity. For instance, he recalls the strange sounds heard on a night walk: 'the language of the ancient earth' (309) or when, with a companion or more often alone, he goes out at dawn into the peaceful Esthwaite valley. By the age of seventeen he has found in the mountains and valleys around him a 'never-failing principle of joy' (450).

Book III concerns Wordsworth's student days at Cambridge. Away from his 'cataracts and mountains' he feels somewhat out of place, finding the academic programme uninspired and getting very angry about the college chapel services he had to attend and which he thought meaningless. Yet he was far from unhappy, discovering 'my heart was social . . . and loved idleness and joy' (235,6). In fact

Wordsworth used this time for wide reading, and speaks of his delight in Chaucer, Shakespeare, Spencer and Milton.

Book IV describes a visit to Hawkshead in the summer vacation which renews his love of the people there and of the place. It is now that he feels himself dedicated to being a poet, and this renewal of 'human-heartedness' and poetic energy is expressed, as so often in this poem, by a particular incident. Late at night, on the way home from a dance, he encounters a solitary man who turns out to be a discharged soldier. They talk, and the man's stoic bearing of poverty and weakness makes an indelible impression.

In Book V, Wordsworth reviews what he 'owed to books in early life' and contrasts the freedom of his education, when he was allowed to read books like *Don Quixote* and *The Arabian Nights*, with the rational, pressurised approach of modern education which deprives the child of the teaching given by Nature and by the imagination. He believes his own upbringing prepared him to encounter the mystery of death and recounts the episode of the drowned man and of a schoolfriend who died young. He also describes a vivid dream of meeting an Arab in the desert, escaping some impending cataclysm and carrying to safety the symbols of science and poetry.

Book VI returns to Cambridge, and Wordsworth mentions again the 'transcendent peace' he finds in geometry. A visit to Yorkshire with his sister is followed by departure 'with a youthful friend' to France, now in the first flush of revolutionary enthusiasm, and across the Alps into Italy.

Book VII reflects upon Wordsworth's life in London, which he shows as a phantasmagoria of disunity and dehumanisation: typically, it is the sudden encounter with a blind beggar which enables him to make sense of the experience. In the next book, too, there is much implicit and explicit comparison between the environment of his own childhood and that offered by the 'enormous city's turbulent world', and he interrupts the chronological sequence to trace his gradual realisation of the interaction between the love of nature and the love of man.

Books IX and X resume the chronological pattern, with Wordsworth's 1791 visit to France. Initially Wordsworth is full of enthusiasm but he watches with growing dismay as the revolutionaries 'become oppressors in their turn'. The final books show Wordsworth's attempts to come to terms with the failure of political hopes, his deep depression and the temptation to yield up 'moral questions in despair' (305). Once again Wordsworth uses a specific episode to crystallise and solve his dilemma.

In Book XIV Wordsworth describes his ascent by night of Snowdon, the highest mountain in Wales, ascending through the mist to the sudden vision of the moon above the clouds. He feels his 'faith in life endless' is restored and that he can at last understand the pattern of his life which he set out to discover in Book I. This is the climax of the poem, followed by his salutations to those whose help has been vital to his achievement of self-knowledge: his wife and sister and, above all, the 'Friend', Coleridge.

2.3 BOOK I: COMMENTARY

I.1–30

Wordsworth had many well-loved examples before him of how to begin an epic poem. Homer and Virgil start by identifying their heroes and promising to tell their story. Milton announces his intention of recounting and explaining the fall of Adam and Eve. Such openings are interwoven with appeals to the Muse of Poetry to inspire the writers before they launch into the narrative proper. Wordsworth's opening is like none of these: he is rejoicing in escape, and an escape so important that it has renewed his life, but what he has escaped from and what kind of liberty he celebrates is suggested, not defined. Typically, the journey he is engaged upon is both factual and metaphorical. The journey to Dove Cottage in Grasmere in 1799 was real enough, and he had recently left the walled city of Goslar and before that the unwalled but equally uncongenial London. It is the metaphorical power of the passage, however, which is its primary importance. It is virtually an exclamation of delight in freedom, dominated by images of air, of unmapped journeys and haunted by echoes of Milton's *Paradise Lost*. This ends with the expulsion of a sad Adam and Eve from Paradise into an earth where they see little comfort: 'The world was all before them, where to choose / Their place of rest, and Providence their guide: / They hand in hand with wandring steps and slow. / Through Eden took their solitarie way'.

Wordsworth is starting his own epic with a matching but contrasted image: for him the earth is not second best and his subject not the fall of man but the exploration of his mind.

The paragraph starts with an exhalation, and the image of air, with its symbolism of freedom, artistic inspiration and of life itself, appears in many different forms – the breeze fans his cheek, brings joy and indeed becomes a being –it is 'half-conscious', it is referred to as 'he', not 'it'; the poet himself becomes a creature of the air (9). The air will provide him (17) with a guide in the 'wandering cloud' – notice how the confidence of 'I cannot miss my way' contrasts with the dying fall of Milton's last line and the precision of the latter's 'Providence' with the instinctual, non-intellectual quality of Wordsworth's guides: 'cloud', 'trackless field . . . floating thing / Upon the river'. The diction echoes the celebration of a freedom to let life take its course: his stay in cities is described in terms of 'escaped', 'discontented', 'pined', 'burthen', 'unnatural', 'heavy weight', 'weary day'. This contrasts sharply with the voice of the open air: 'wanderings', 'mountings', and the last three lines manage to produce a swift topographical vision: 'road', 'pathway', 'field', 'hill', 'down', 'river'. The sense of exhilarating freedom is reflected in the reiterated questions: anything is possible now that he has escaped the suffocation of the oppressive city, which, by the end of the paragraph, we realise is also an image of the 'Burthen of my own unnatural self'. Wordsworth rejoices in the prospect of rediscovering his real self in the freedom of the natural world.

I.31–45

The images of freedom in the first paragraph – breeze, breathing, floating – are now given a new turn as 'the sweet breath of heaven' he feels blowing upon him is answered by a 'corresponding breeze' of inspiration within himself. Indeed he knows that it is only this 'gift' of inspiration that will enable him to make use of his new-found freedom. He delays identifying this gift until the last line of the paragraph, and the images associated with it become increasingly powerful and demanding. It is God-given since it 'consecrates' his joy in natural freedom, and its gentle movement quickens rapidly into a 'tempest'. Wordsworth describes its energy as 'redundant' (super-abundant) with a strength so overwhelming that it is 'vexing its own creation'. This strange phrase bears the metrical emphasis of an initial inversion of stress; it is the climax to a long sentence and brings an abrupt mid-line stop. That Wordsworth had difficulty in finding the right words here is reflected in manuscript variants: the 1805 version has an enlightening extra phrase. There the wind of inspiration first passes over 'things which it has made' before becoming a 'vexing', i.e. violently agitated, tempest. The suggestion is that Wordsworth's new-found inspiration is so strong that he sees everything he has written before in a different light.

This power of transformation is caught up by the next image, which develops from the two forces of lines 33 and 35: this is of warmth-bringing winds, 'congenial powers', to end the winter frost and renew creativity. 'Frost', like the earlier 'city', provides an image of Wordsworth's frustration before he saw his vocation clearly. Now he eagerly anticipates that his 'dear liberty' will be filled with writing. To achieve this he will need a life which is active yet with time for meditation, and which will be given its pattern by his poetry, a vocation implicitly compared to a religious one by the use of 'service . . . matins . . . vespers'. The first paragraph was an upsurge of joy in freedom won at last. This balances it with a commitment to work through 'active days'. Exactly what this work will be is still unclear, but it is prefigured as unsettling, energetic, unpredictable and as demanding as religion.

I.46-58

Usually Wordsworth wrote poetry well after the original experience which he recalled later 'in tranquillity', as Coleridge well knew. This is why he speaks here of how unusual was the spontaneous overflowing of relief and joy that expressed itself immediately in these lines when he was on his way to Grasmere in the winter of 1799. In the earlier version he actually says that they came to him 'Even in the very words which I have here / Recorded', but his passion for revision meant he had to alter this to 'that would not be forgotten'. Again a religious aura is given to the poetry with 'prophecy', and to the poet's vocation with 'priestly robe . . . renovated spirit . . . holy services'. The vocabulary carries an echo of the kind of spiritual journal popular among Puritans (see section 4.1) with its concern for conversion. Wordsworth's ability to turn what has happened immediately into verse – 'my own voice' – encourages him, but even more important is his awareness of the deeper quality of the experience itself. The description of this (56) has a curious aural effect, since the idea of echo is reproduced in the stresses, and the central vowel sound of 'imperfect' does in fact echo 'internal'. Wordsworth is saying here, as he often does, that language can never adequately capture experience – but at this moment both experience and what he can write about it give him hope for the future.

I.59–131

Wordsworth returns to the account of his journey and puts aside for the moment the stresses of composition. He finds an ideal resting place among a grove of oak trees and remains there from two o'clock until nearly sunset. The autumn weather is calm and sunny and the place is very peaceful, the only noise being the occasional sound of an acorn dropping through dead leaves to the bare ground. At last he sets off again to the valley (Grasmere) where he has chosen to live, and as he walks on through the 'splendid evening' he tries once more to capture his experience in poetry. But after a few starts, he finds inspiration has left him; he compares his inability to find the right words to an Aeolian harp which is 'defrauded', i.e. deprived of wind. Aeolian harps were very popular from the eighteenth century onwards: a sounding box with strings stretched upon it was hung, perhaps near a window, where the current of air would produce notes. Here, however, the wind of inspiration has ceased to pluck any response from Wordsworth's own 'sounding box'. He accepts this temporary inability serenely, feeling that the 'present joy' of the day is what matters and that calm passivity – a 'Sabbath' – is to be welcomed as gladly as the sudden urge to write.

Once settled in his 'hermitage' (107), Dove Cottage, where he would live with his sister Dorothy from 1799 to 1808, he finds an 'unbroken cheerfulness' in all the delightful small concerns of life: of practical matters here he gives no details, though these are easily discovered in Dorothy's journals and his own letters – details about neighbours, gardening and other jobs around the tiny cottage and endless huge walks in all weathers. But what he returns to now in this poem is the fluctuation between his intense urge to write and the 'impediments' which seem to prevent this. First of all (114–18) he records his longing to get to work, possibly reading or re-reading in case he starts to forget what he already knows. But he also has 'higher hopes', and these are the desire to find what T. S. Eliot, the poet and critic, called an 'objective correlative'. This rather cumbersome phrase means the discovery of some episode or event or even objects which the poet can use to evoke in the reader an emotion of equal intensity to that which originally drove him to write. Wordsworth plays with the idea (123) that the feelings that will not leave him in peace might be made vivid to the reader by using what he calls here 'airy phantasies'. We may assume that he is thinking in terms of a narrative historical poem centred round one of the heroes he mentions later (110–20). But his enthusiasm for his 'noble theme' always seems to die away, in spite of the 'bud promise of the past', that absolute assurance that he can write. This passage is full of images of frustration: the dawning light disappears, he is mocked by a sky that does not 'ripen' and the energy lying in 'gladly grapple' is frittered away by the oppressively regular metre of the paragraph's last line and a half, and the suggestion of being shackled by 'impediments' that recur on all sides.

I.132–45

At such times Wordsworth contemplates temporarily abandoning his plans of writing a great work and turning his hand to 'humble industry'. Perhaps this means shorter poems like those in *The Lyrical Ballads* which he had published with Coleridge. Certainly it is to Coleridge that his thoughts immediately turn here – the 'dear Friend' who he feels is one of the few who can share his problems. There is a buried reference in the next few lines to Shakespeare's *A Midsummer Night's Dream*, which classes together the 'lunatic, the lover and the poet' since they are 'of imagination all compact'. Wordsworth acquiesces in the implicit unease of the poet's lot: 'unruly time', 'distress', 'unmanageable thought' suggest the intense unease of 'frustrated creation'. This is picked up by the image of the dove. In Milton's *Paradise Lost* the creation of the universe stems from the Holy Spirit which 'Dove-like' broods over chaos and creates order. So too the human mind reduces the chaos of its thought to order by brooding and meditation. But the process is not simple; it is interrupted by almost unbearable pressures. Wordsworth here (142–3) images it in the sudden feverish disquiet of the 'innocent bird': he shares that 'passion' and knows it is necessary to creation. It will only be blameworthy if he lets it last too long.

Much later in *The Prelude* (VI.635–6) when he is describing the wild mountains and wilder weather of the Alps, Wordsworth speaks again of the necessary tension between serenity and disquiet to produce creation: 'Tumult and peace, the darkness and the light / Were all alike the workings of one mind, the features / Of the same face, blossoms upon one tree . . .'

I.146–269

In the same way that Milton had prepared himself to write *Paradise Lost*, Wordsworth reviews his own abilities. He is confident that he possesses four of the necessary gifts. What he lacks, however, is a clear lead as to his subject, and he passes in review a long list of possibilities, mostly to do with heroes of liberty and nationalism and ending with yet another reference to the 'philosophic song / Of Truth' that fascinates him but which he keeps nervously postponing until he is older. So Wordsworth remains in miserable indecision, wondering if it would not be better to forget his ambition and simply delight in his life at Grasmere: but always he is conscious that he can and ought to utilise his powers.

This is a very long paragraph and it invites discussion in at least three ways: Wordsworth's estimate of his own poetic equipment, the multiplicity of stories which he considers and rejects, and the way both structure and language reveal his state of mind in these early years at Dove Cottage.

First of his poetic gifts is his 'vital soul', the lively force of imagination which shapes all experience. Next he puts what he calls 'general Truths'. This phrase, which helps to illuminate Wordsworth's meaning, is taken from Samuel Johnson, who in his novel, *Rasselas*, describes the qualities a poet must possess. The poet must study every aspect of man's behaviour and from this achieve understanding of 'general and transcendental truths'. It is this understanding of the way people work, and the freedom from the prejudice of 'his age and country' which makes the poet a man apart. Wordsworth clearly sees this analytic, intellectual ability as a necessary 'agent' to help him discriminate between imaginative truth and the illusions with which the chances of private life and public events can cloud any judgement relying on sensibility without rationality. Wordsworth's third qualification for writing is also illuminated by Johnson, where the poet 'ranged mountains and deserts for images', and we realise that these 'external things, Forms, Images' are in fact the landscapes peopled with individual human beings that we most readily associate with Wordsworth's poetry. Finally Wordsworth adds (in a somewhat dismissive way) the 'toil' expended on developing the technique of writing poetry.

Wordsworth's hesitation about his subject matter is presented directly to the reader in the detailed account that now follows. He is thinking in terms of a narrative epic centring round a 'little band' of characters to whom he could give contemporary and future fame (164–5). Milton, in a similar dilemma about subject, had considered, then rejected, a theme of heroic chivalry, possibly about Arthur and his knights. Should Wordsworth pick up this theme? Or he could write – as the Tudor poet, Spenser, did – on a more peaceful aspect of chivalry, the pursuit of excellence against wicked enchantments. The 1850 version gives this possibility sixteen lines against four in 1805, and adds a decidedly more moral tone. Wordsworth then turns to yet another literary source, the historian Edward Gibbon, and wonders about two of the stories to be found there: Mithridates was defeated by Rome in the first century BC, fled northwards from the Black Sea, and may have been the ancestor of Odin and the barbaric tribes who would later cause Rome's own downfall. An ally of Mithridates was Sertorius. There is a legend that his followers fled to the Canary Islands and only lost their independence when the Spanish invaded in the fifteenth century. Both these subjects show how Wordsworth's mind is moving towards a story illustrating the struggle for liberty, and the next possibility (200–5) is to invent a character who fights some historic tyranny. In this context he remembers an actual Frenchman, Dominique de Gourges, who did just this, going to Florida in 1568 to avenge the massacre of his countrymen by Spaniards. There is the Swedish struggle for independence against the Danes, when Gustavus enlisted the mining community in his aid. Then, possibly because of Wordsworth's 1803 tour of Scotland with Dorothy, he thinks of William Wallace, whose death in the cause of Scottish nationalism inspired his country. Finally he considers a story with the same serious intention but concerning someone like himself.

Yet none of these varied narratives attracts him for long; he is always drawn towards a different sort of poem, which will work out a philosophy to cast light upon 'our daily life'. The word 'thoughtfully' is important here, for it suggests that the poem would stem from reason symbolised for Wordsworth by 'the Orphean lyre', instead of that mysterious spontaneous power he was welcoming at the beginning of this book. On the other hand, Wordsworth feels he should wait until he is older and with more experience before embarking upon such a philosophical poem.

Thus Wordsworth is left in the same dilemma, never quite sure of his own motivation for delay. Lines 238–49 both identify the conflicting forces that bewilder him, and the breaking up of lines, the Miltonian antithesis of phrase against phrase, suggest his painfully divided feelings. He cannot estimate the strength of his impulse to write. It may be very strong (240), or perhaps his lack of power to accomplish this writing deceives him with a 'vague longing': he cannot distinguish between a fear of his great task and a sensible caution (241), between thorough preparation and endless postponement (242). He does not even know if his delay shows a reasonable modesty or a 'subtle selfishness'. This phrase he develops in the next four lines: it shows itself as an inability to write anything (246) or to face up to his true subject when he meets it (249). That is, he is finding any excuse for doing nothing and he worries if this may be because of a deep fear of his own inadequacy. Possibly he should abandon his ambition to write, surrender to the delights of the 'rural walks' around him, and live solely in the present: that would be better than to be caught in this quandary between aspiration and paralysis. Yet such surrender would, he knows, be wrong, as is shown by his reference to the parable of the false steward who took his master's goods and gave no return (Matthew 25:14–30).

The style of this long, 'baffled' paragraph reflects Wordsworth's troubled state of mind as he searches for his true poetic voice. The tone is set by 'arduous', 'rigorous', 'inquisition' of 147–8 and even the 'cheering' review of his gifts is overcast by the succession of negative forms he uses here, while the phrase about his technical abilities 'won perhaps with toil' seems out of key with the spontaneity he hymned at the opening of Book I.

This feeling of being ill-at-ease is communicated in the sheer detail of the list of considered and then rejected themes that give Wordsworth brief hope and then recurring disappointment. The reader shares the poet's feeling of not knowing which way to turn – a predicament verbally caught in the jostling alternatives of lines 238–49. The discomfort of Wordsworth's state is emphasised too by a succession of painful images: his poetry becomes a 'burden', his days are passed 'in contradiction', he is betrayed (244) duped (247) 'baffled and plagued' (257), his mind turns traitor (258), he finds his thought 'hollow'. Then he reaches the monosyllabic despair of 'This is my lot', where the 'repose' he seeks is mere 'listlessness' and his perplexity is, though painful, 'vain' because it is 'unprofitable'. The final lines carry a bleak vision not only of death but of judgement on his waste of talent.

It is at this moment – and significantly in the middle of a line – when, with the suddenness of revelation, all Wordsworth's self-doubt about his powers and confusion about his subject vanish. He must turn to nature: the nature of his childhood and the nature in which that childhood developed. The traditional epic themes are not for him. In the poem it is like coming out of a long oppressive tunnel into the sunlight, and the dramatic change that comes with the next paragraph makes clear just what has been the function of this passage. In its complexity and worried detail, the eroding uncertainty of its antithesis and the vocabulary of emotional discomfort it acts as a perfect foil to the bounding joy and serenity that will follow.

I.269–300

The transition here is abrupt. In fact this paragraph, little changed, was the opening of the original two-part *Prelude* written in 1799. Wordsworth was finding it difficult to get on with the purely 'philosophical' poem that Coleridge was urging him to write. In order to understand what was holding him back from his uncongenial task he turned to his own childhood with this question: was it his upbringing, his environment that made it difficult for him to write? What immediately happens is that the force of recollection sweeps him away from his own questioning – and this happens in all the existing versions of the poem – into a sustained celebration of his childhood and boyhood. In typically epic style, like Milton in the second paragraph of *Paradise Lost*, he asks a question but will allow the poem itself to answer.

There could not be a greater contrast with the frustrations of the previous paragraph than the image of the onward flowing river whose music is of such power that it 'composed my thoughts': now the poet need only be passive instead of painfully struggling, and draw upon this promise of the serenity to be found in nature. Wordsworth remembers the course of the river: flowing down from the mountains it passed beneath Cockermouth Castle and then beside their garden; the sounds of its waterfalls and shallows are his earliest memory, associated with his nurse's lullaby and his dreams; his memories of the freedom of his childhood echo the sense of freedom and escape.

Central to the passage is the unity between the child and the natural world. The river is made human, spoken of as 'he', not 'it', who 'loved' to add his voice to that of the nurse, 'a tempting playmate'. The child plunges repeatedly into this loved element, as he does into the yellow ragwort which seems as tall as trees to the five-year-old. He is equally at home with the hugeness of Skiddaw, which he could see nine miles to the east. Just as the child 'basked in the sun', so the mountain is 'Bronzed with deepest radiance'. The climactic image is that of a child of nature, naked and alone on the earth from which he has been born, playing not with other humans, but with the 'thunder shower' – like a Red Indian child, says Wordsworth, a 'naked savage'.

To any post-Rousseau Romantic, this image meant freedom from the corrupting rationalising influences of civilisation and union with the formative powers of nature.

I.301–25

The next picture of young Wordsworth is four years later. Now transported to Hawkshead Grammar School in the Valley of Esthwaite, he still has great freedom. In the autumn he spends 'half the night' scouring the hills to inspect the traps he has laid for woodcocks. These were much in demand, we learn from contemporary sources. This sport is his 'joy', but he is conscious that his activity is out of key with the serene night landscape, and when he occasionally filches a bird from someone else's trap ('toils'), this unease turns into a feeling of menace from the hills around.

The opening of the paragraph carries over the image of the child in the thunder shower (300) to that of the sowing of fruitful seed, but inverted initial stresses and alliteration direct the reader's attention to the idea that nature's education includes fear. It is a very special kind of fear that Wordsworth is describing, and his choice of this particular example carried marked contrasts to the previous scene. It is a frosty night instead of a summer's day, he has a lot of traps ('springes') over his shoulder, he is now in a hurry ('scudding', 'anxious'). He is no longer one with nature but a trouble to the peace, and the unthinking joy of the child is replaced by 'strong desire'. This is a splendidly accurate account of a boy single-mindedly pursuing his current passion. It would be a mistake to assume Wordsworth is shaking his head over his predatory former self, as his touches of parody of epic style reveal ('captive', 'prey').

What Wordsworth records is the unignorable power of his surroundings. Even though the boy seems wholly absorbed by his trapping, he is uneasily aware that the quietude of the night sky belittles his own business, and when he has stolen from another's trap, guilt for the petty theft is transformed into a primitive terror of unknown forces – breathings, sound, motion, steps which are terrifyingly unconnected to any physical presence. Nature here controls through fear as well as beauty.

I.326–39

In the spring, Wordsworth and his friends go bird's-nesting, leaving the cultivated ('cultured') valley far below as they climb the 'naked crag' and 'perilous ridge' which surround it. The object – to get birds' eggs – is acknowledged as petty, but the result ('end') was not, for the experience of hanging precariously perched, holding on by tiny crevices in the 'slippery rock' and only kept there at all by the force of the wind, fills the boy with awe.

In all these three paragraphs, Nature has a different voice – the loving murmurings of the Derwent (271), the terrifying, pursuing breathings from the hills (323), and now the 'strange utterance of the loud dry wind'. He has been in the water, on the hills, and is now in the air, and the dread which ended the previous paragraph is replaced here by a feeling of such strangeness that can only be adequately saluted by exclamation. Twice he breaks into a exhalation of wonder – 'Oh!' is echoed by 'alone' and 'Blow', and the amazed 'With what strange utterance' is repeated in the final line. The paragraph has a powerful suggestion of physicality: the exclamations suggest the efforts of the poet to convey something beyond words but also the desperate panting of the climber. The force of the wind is such that the climber is 'suspended by the blast' which is 'shouldering' the crags themselves; we hear its noise (337) and see its strength exerted on the clouds. The rapid transition in the last two lines from sky to earth and back to clouds has a vertiginous effect prefaced by 'hung' and 'suspended'. The desperate hold of fingers on rock is suggested by the alliteration of 'fissures', 'slippery', 'ill sustained' and the fragility of 'tufts of grass'. Such a passage as this demonstrates Wordsworth's power to make his writing echo the experience itself.

I.340–56

Wordsworth pauses here between two incidents from his youth and looks back as well as forward in the poem. He has given us in lines 235–69 an example of his 'vexations, lassitudes', followed by the totally different element of his boyhood experiences. Here he reflects upon the strange way in which such different elements are combined together to make an individual (340–3) and marvels that his own existence, at its best, should now be so calm. He is conscious that he owes this peace of mind to the way Nature has formed him and speaks here of three different kinds of 'visitings' – those which brought no sense of fear, those which were startling but not frightening, like the summer lightning, and those which would be so threatening that they would haunt his very dreams. The bird-trapping exploit had a flavour of such fear, but he is going on to give a far more terrifying example.

Once again Wordsworth uses a metaphor from music to illustrate his theme of the strange way in which discord can be resolved by 'inscrutable Workmanship' into harmony. (See Section 5.1 for the various versions of these lines.)

I.357–400

Wordsworth launches immediately into an example of 'severer intervention' by Nature. The 1805 version makes it clear that he was staying by himself for the night in Patterdale and therefore in country strange to him. Wandering out from the village inn late in the evening, he sees a little boat on the shores of Lake Ullswater and decides to go for a row. Keeping straight by looking steadily at the summit he is rowing away from, suddenly (as it seems to him) another 'huge peak', probably Black Cray, rears up behind and, of course, as he rows harder to get away, he sees it as bigger and bigger. He turns back, restores the boat to its moorings and goes home to bed. The experience left him troubled in the extreme. Both by day and by night he was haunted by a consciousness of strange, non-human, powerful forces which left him bereft in a land of spiritual darkness.

This famous story is easy to misinterpret. Of course it is true that he should not have taken the boat without permission and he admits that 'it was an act of stealth', but it would be misplaced to view the episode as a simple little moral tale. It presents to the reader two strongly contrasted states of mind. The first is of a highly wrought state of excitement, of daring and delight: Wordsworth is in holiday mood, alone by a strange lake in the moonlight with the boat awaiting him as boats did in endless romances he had read. His senses are alive to the intense beauty of the scene – the glittering, ever-changing effect of his oars upon the moonlit water – and to the delight of physical effort: 'Like one who rows / Proud of his skill', 'lustily I dipped my oars', 'I rose upon the stroke', 'heaving through the water'. The boat itself is transformed into an 'elfin pinnace', 'a swan'. Then, exactly at the mid-point of the story, the nature of Wordsworth's fantasy changes from delight to terror as his vivid imagination endows the emerging peak with living but not human attributes. It is huge and black (he sees it against the grey, starry sky), it lifts its head, becoming even bigger as he desperately tries to row away, it is grim and full of purpose (voluntary power), it 'towered up' and in nightmare style 'strode after him'. The boy Wordsworth would have realised with his rational mind why the peak seemed to grow, since all his life he had lived among mountains, but reason is replaced by an imagination fuelled by the unfamiliar time and place, a feeling of guilt, and a ferment of literary ideas – the mysterious ogres and giants of chivalric tales as well as a more sinister echo in the 'grim shape' of Milton's figure of Death itself. The effect on the boy is shown in both immediate and deferred results. The oars and the moonlit water in which he had been taking such pleasure transform: the oars are 'trembling' now and the water 'silent'. This word is picked up by the alliteration of 'stole' and contrasts with the physical exultation of his earlier rowing, while 'covert' suggests hiding and refuge. The delayed effect is imaged in ten lines which bristle with a variety of negative forms. The reiterated 'no' is used to banish all the 'pleasant images' and colours of his beloved familiar world, as 'not' deletes the 'living men'. Instead, there is a succession of 'forms', all the more awesome because they are 'unknown', 'dim and undetermined', bringing 'darkness', 'solitude', 'blank desertion'. Like the 'huge peak', these unknowable forms will not let him alone but 'moved slowly' (notice the two heavy syllables which weigh down the centre of this line) through his conscious and unconscious mind.

What the adult Wordsworth has achieved here is to record exactly the workings of his boyish imagination on that evening and to exemplify what he will speak of in his next paragraph as the intwining of passions, here joy and terror, both activated by the living world around him.

I.401–24

The previous paragraph recorded both outer and inner events meticulously from the boy's viewpoint: here the voice is different. It is the mature Wordsworth, with a hymn of thanksgiving for the way in which his mind has been formed. It is interesting to compare the 1850 opening of this paragraph with the original 1799 version, where Wordsworth addresses 'ye beings of the hills / And ye that walk the woods and open heaths / By moon or starlight'. The gentle pantheism here is in strong contrast to 1850, with its firm deistic invocation in the first line, and with the impacted meaning of the second, which seems to mean that human philosophy has given to the notion of eternity the name 'soul'.

The shaping influences of nature, continuously present from Wordsworth's earliest recollections (405), have linked his feelings not with the works of man, as they would if he had been town-bred, but with 'enduring things' (mountains, fields, lakes, sky). Because his human thoughts and feelings have been developed against a perspective of such enduring nature, he has learnt to recognise how pain and fear, in its religious sense of awe, bear witness to the 'grandeur' of man's existence (414) in summer, noon and night, in woods, fields, hills and by the lake. Wordsworth gratefully records the omnipresent nature of this 'fellowship', this 'intercourse'. It is associated with solitude and often with a feeling of near dread: the 'trembling lake' readily recalls the 'trembling oars' of the boat episode, and the November mists and 'gloomy hills' remind us not to imagine Wordsworth's vision of nature in a rosily romantic way.

I.425–63

From the summer of the previous line Wordsworth moves vigorously into an account of winter skating, a sport at which he excelled. It is a composite picture: the cottage windows suggest Colthouse or Esthwaite, but the crags and cliff suggest Windermere. The time is twilight, six o'clock; the cottage windows are ablaze with the reflected light of the setting sun, while the eastern sky is already 'sparkling' with stars. The skaters play at hare and hounds and even have a hunting horn which adds to the din, while the near precipices and far hills return an echo. Often Wordsworth would turn away from the tumult and the crowd to chase the reflection of a star or, after reaching great speed, stop so suddenly that the cliffs on either hand still seemed to go spinning on as though he could actually witness the revolution of the earth itself, as though the earth itself had joined in with the intense activity of the skaters, until gradually the illusion ceased and all was still. (For detailed comment on this passage, see Section 6.3.)

I.464–75

As in the earlier passage (401–24) Wordsworth turns again from the brilliant evocation of his boyhood to salute the forces that have made him what he is. The invocation with its prophetic 'ye' is not meant to suggest general personifications but particular numinous experiences. Most of the paragraph takes the form of a question, for Wordsworth cannot be certain that the extraordinary 'ministry' of all these forces was intended for a special purpose, but it is clear that the question is rhetorical, answering itself: such a prolonged experience, manifested in so many different places cannot have been a 'vulgar' (commonplace) or ordinary matter. What has the 'ministry' achieved?

To Wordsworth the 'surface of the universal earth' is alive, perpetually in motion like the sea, suffused with the vivid presence of these actual forces which have impressed the 'characters' of everything Wordsworth has ever felt upon 'caves and trees, upon the woods and hills'. There is a bare and powerful simplicity in this line, as there is in the earlier invocation of sky, earth, hills and lonely places. The fourfold shape of each is then echoed in 'the triumph and delight, with hope and fear' (474). Wordsworth has already established that these forces appear to conflict but in fact supplement each other, but the loose broken nature of the line itself reinforces the powerful image of movement in the final half-line.

I.475–8, 479–98

The opening sentence links the general theme of the previous paragraph with more specific examples of the way the young Wordsworth has been 'haunted' among 'all his boyish sports' by the feeling of shared vitality with nature. He is emphatic that this theme will be 'not uselessly employed'. In case any critical reader might expect an epic to treat only those traditional tales he had earlier listed, this, he insists, is his right theme, picking up from every season of the year those experiences that had formed his mind. The ease and fluidity with which he moves among these 'delights' contrasts strongly with the impersonal, almost mechanical listing of lines 166–220.

The beauty of the countryside where he spent his boyhood was only equalled by the delight he had in his friends. He remembers gathering hazelnuts in autumn, fishing in the summer along rivers deeply overhung by trees (488), and above all the excitement of flying kites, sometimes in good weather from the hill-tops, sometimes, when the wind was strong, from the meadows.

It is typical of the apparent spontaneity of Wordsworth's writing that we do not at first notice how his recollection moves from earth to water and then to air and sky, how the boy's activity in both fishing and kite flying, intensely enjoyed for its own sake, also exemplifies the equally powerful life in nature itself. The 'rod and line' obviously do not bring home much fish: instead the 'noisy crew' are 'led on' further and further 'all the green summer' into yet remoter valleys, as though enchanted. The kite-flying evokes precise physical memories – the 'pull' at the string (495) and equally the unpredictable dashing of the kite to the ground. Visual image, 'high among the fleecy clouds', is equalled by metrical illusion of violence with the two heavy stresses of 'Dashed headlong'. The cheerful crowd of boys did not reflect then upon this manifestation of nature's power, but Wordsworth gradually realises from the vividness of his memory how such things had 'made me what I am'.

I.499–543

From the gusty outdoor excitement of kite-flying, Wordsworth turns to the 'lowly cottage' where he lived with a small group of fellow-pupils and vividly recalls their games when rain or frost kept them indoors. The cottages, like the outside world, had their own 'ministration', for they gave a sense of happiness and security with their 'plain comforts . . . by the warm peat-fire'. The first game described is noughts and crosses: Wordsworth and his 'noisy crew' would have called it tick-tack-toe, but the elaborate description here is a joke. Indeed, this passage about games becomes in itself a literary game. The cards are given the same mock heroic personalities that the earlier poets, William Cowper and Alexander Pope, had already used, and words like 'thick-ribbed', here presumably suggesting well-thumbed cards, are slyly taken from Milton's description of the ice in Hell. Wordsworth-as-adult enjoys the way he is playing with other poems in the same way that Wordsworth-as-schoolboy had made the usual jokes about the peculiar faces on the playing cards. Even so, there is at times an underlying seriousness, recalling his preoccupation with those who were displaced or solitary: lines 518–19 recall his own encounter one night with an impoverished discharged soldier. In the middle of a line, as in the middle of an 'eager game', comes the sudden awareness of the world outside, the 'incessant rain' or the extraordinary noise of the cracking ice on nearby Esthwaite. The sound of the air bursting from under the ice is like wolves, and the image suddenly transplants the reader from the warm companionable cottage to the frozen Baltic and the wildest and most desolate aspects of nature. It is typical that Wordsworth should juxtapose the two in this way.

I.544–58

Wordsworth pauses in his recollections to distinguish between two kinds of influence which have formed him. The first he calls 'extrinsic' because it has operated or originated outside himself: in the 1799 version he calls it 'collateral'. In all the adventures which had stored his boyish mind with such 'sublime or fair' recollections, and which he has so far recounted, Nature was acting upon him while he had been unconscious at the time of what was happening. But there had also been a force at work from within his own nature. This was the spontaneous reaction of his senses which he associates with the natural 'affinities' between the new-born child and its surroundings, that feeling of being at home in its world which gives it joy in living – 'a bond of union between life and joy'. He characterises this instinctive, intrinsic sense of belonging as joyous, simple and calm, and makes the same link here between a child's sensuous awareness and its spiritual quality (in this poem 'intellectual' carries the meaning of spiritual).

The opening here is not very smooth. Most of the paragraph transitions are more ably engineered, but the line (based on one of Milton's) stayed the same through all three versions and must reflect Wordsworth's need to balance how 'sedulous' (diligent, busy) he has been in describing one kind of influence, by describing another equally important and perhaps ('if I err not') even more essential.

I.559–66, 567–80

The opening turns back to Wordsworth's memories of himself at ten years old. It is typical that it is quite unlike the opening of the previous paragraph. Instead of the complex construction of a borrowed style, there is the immediate simple affirmation of 'Yes, I remember.' What he remembers is this sensuous delight in beauty – a delight so intense that he drinks it in, it becomes an 'organic' part of himself. It is primaeval, 'old as creation' and, as often with Wordsworth, he speaks in terms of water – the wreaths of mist on the lakes, the 'plain of waters' reflecting the gathering of 'impending' clouds.

With the next paragraph this vision of water enlarges to the sea, viewed from the coast of Cumberland and at a particular time. The dusk of evening is being broken by moonlight. As the moon rises, it first touches the higher ground, 'the shepherd's hut on distant hills', and this light is 'welcome'. But such ideas or 'fancies' as this do not occur to the little boy: he only sees what is before him, nor has he yet been conditioned to associate quietness and peace with such a scene. He stands watching the huge expanse – 'many a league' – of moonlit water, and he gathers 'pleasure like a bee among the flowers'. The pleasure is intense, he misses nothing: 'every hair breadth in that field of light' feeds him as the mists did in I.564.

Light and water are very primitive things – myth has it that light was the first creation, and what Wordsworth is saying here is that the child's response to this intensely beautiful scene of the moon rising over the sea is as instinctive as eating.

The background to the adult Wordsworth's thinking is the theory of the eighteenth-century philosopher David Hartley that the operations of our minds derive from the senses. In time these primary sensations are built upon by associations from further experiences, and this forms the basis of our understanding. Here, however, the child's perceptions are still unalloyed by associations – they are primitive in their single-mindedness. The sense of total freedom is conveyed by the huge vista of waters where the boy misses not one iota of the sparkling light.

I.581–612

Wordsworth clearly desires to work out for himself and the reader just how his consciousness of nature developed. This is shown when he pauses to repeat, and yet, in the complexity of the two long sentences which constitute the paragraph, to mirror the difficulty of establishing a true account of this journey into his past life.

There is the paramount difficulty of remembering what one has forgotten, and the first sentence attempts just this. It opens with a reference to the intensity of his 'vulgar' (everyday) delights as a child and the speed with which these were forgotten. They were 'like a temper', violent but soon over, and 'giddy', i.e. excited but ephemeral. Contrast with the impression of stillness and hugeness at the end of the previous paragraph is striking, but Wordsworth uses the same image of light, here like the sudden flashing of a shield, to claim that 'even then' revelation did briefly come. Nor was everything forgotten, since the ordinary, commonplace face of Nature spoke 'remembered things': sometimes these were impressed upon him by what seemed chance. Wordsworth compares it to the way malignant fairies supposedly cause the wrong people to fall in love (the reference is probably to Shakespeare's *A Midsummer Night's Dream*). Yet subsequent experience has demonstrated that a good purpose was served by the apparently haphazard process, since the sights thus impressed upon him and whose significance he did not realise then ('lifeless . . . doomed to sleep') would inspire him ('impregnate and elevate the mind') when he was older, in 'maturer seasons'.

The second sentence looks again at the interaction of memory and forgetfulness. The powerful operation of the senses can appear to be forgotten, but the landscape evoking the experience remained vividly before the mind's eye, especially since Wordsworth saw it anew every day. To these images, both remembered and actual, the 'frequently repeated' experiences of fear and pleasure (of the kind he had already described in the poem) gradually lent a host of new associations. Even experiences totally forgotten nevertheless left a nucleus of 'representative feelings' to increase the power that the landscape had upon him, 'fastened' as it was to his affections by these 'invisible links'.

The movement of the paragraph provides the pattern of a cumulative process. It spans time, from the 'child's pursuits' through the promise of 'maturer seasons' to the bonding, in the final lines, of experiencer and the world he has experienced. It could be seen as an exemplification of Hartley's doctrine of associations, and the three-fold repetition of 'by' gives a suggestion of scientific objectivity. Yet this objectivity is balanced by the labyrinthine clausal structure with its elusive main clauses, by the distracting, centripetal images which lead away from the main thought line (584,586,590) and by the hedging 'yet' and 'if' which appear in both sentences. The complication of Wordsworth's task is shown to be far removed from the neatness of any abstract theory.

I.612–36

With this paragraph the tone eases and simplifies into direct colloquy with the reader – the 'O Friend!' is both Coleridge and us. Wordsworth asks for sympathy, patience and understanding with this roundabout journey he has chosen towards the 'work of glory' promised in the opening of the Book. There is a certain disingenuousness in the way Wordsworth hopes he has not been 'misled' by the happy memories of his early years to start his poem in this way. The whole impetus of the poem so far has been to demonstrate that he knows that this is his right subject. However, he speaks in apologetic vein, since he cannot be sure that his memories are real: such far-off things, like flowers, cannot survive, though it is typical that he remembers the joy such things gave him. In the 1805 version the flower image was specific. He compared his deceptive memory to 'Planting my snowdrops among winter snows' which catches the sense of life at its very beginning, and also the deceptiveness of recollection since snowdrops could be confused with snow, one white mingling with another white.

Wordsworth is confident of Coleridge's sympathy – indeed, the heavy alliteration of line 620 sounds like a shared joke though the meaning is serious enough: the ideal reader will realise that though his 'tale' is about childhood, it is of central importance, the reverse of 'fond and feeble'. What Wordsworth has hoped to do by this retrospect is to regain some of the energy that he had in his earlier years (622), become more single-minded (623), understand himself better, and help Coleridge understand him. He hopes, too (624–6), that he will find himself spurred on to proceed with *The Recluse* (235). However, whether any of these aims will be achieved or not, he is confident that Coleridge will understand his desire to stay with his present theme of recollected childhood.

Indeed, Wordsworth seems to pass on responsibility for delaying work on a philosophical poem to the fascination exercised upon him by his present 'song' which he describes as 'loth to quit / Those recollected hours'. The terms in which he speaks of the subject of his early life – 'charm . . . visionary . . . lovely forms and sweet sensations' suggest that he is under enchanted compulsion to explore this vision of 'remotest infancy'. The sweetness of the phraseology leaves us in no doubt that this subject attracts him much more than the 'honourable toil' of the projected philosophical poem which has already caused him so much uneasiness. The terms he uses concerning this ('spur . . . toil') derive from Milton's writing about poetic fame in Lycidas: 'Fame is the spur that clear spirit doth raise . . . / To scorn delight and live laborious days'. This paragraph makes it clear that, for the time at least, Wordsworth is opting for a subject that brings nothing but delight.

So the course ahead is clear. The liberty Wordsworth was celebrating at the beginning of the Book is now reconciled with the purpose he has been so earnestly seeking. He has regained his vitality and his confidence and will go forward with the 'story of my life'. The language he uses relaxes into the simplest phrases – 'The road lies plain before me' – and we hear the echo of the opening image of a journey where 'The earth is all before me'. Now a map for the journey has been achieved, and the road will lead Wordsworth back into his past. Until Wordsworth has succeeded in charting the forces that have formed himself, the 'ampler argument' of *The Recluse* might make him 'discomforted and lost', so that must wait until later.

2.4   BOOK II: COMMENTARY

II.1–46

Wordsworth turns again to Coleridge, his 'friend' upon this journey back through his life. He has already sought in his childhood for some of the sources of his love of nature and how he recalls his boyhood, when this love was unconsciously sustained by, for instance, the freedom of the games they played in summer at Hawkshead until long after most of the village had gone to bed. The single-minded delight of those days is contrasted with the situation of the adult who cannot, however much he tries, give to the pursuit of intellect, virtue, duty and truth the spontaneous eagerness he had when young, since the adult is inevitably conscious of the division between mind and body. Yet so intense is Wordsworth's memory of the carefree, unthinking existence of the past that he sometimes seems to be both boy and man – 'two consciousnesses'. He recollects a huge stone which used to be in the middle of the market square. This was the centre of all the village sports, as well as the place where an old woman had kept a little stall for sixty years, as he knows his boyhood friends will remember. But on a recent visit (probably with his brother, John, and Coleridge in 1799) Wordsworth had discovered that the rock had disappeared and some of their playground had been supplanted by a 'smart Assembly-room'.

It is right that Book II should start with a salutation to Coleridge as Wordsworth's close companion, for the emphasis throughout will be on community and fellowship, as this opening memory of his schoolboy games promises. The phrase 'though leaving much unvisited' is a true picture of a journey, whether actual or in memory, for time does not allow completeness in either case: here the reader notices the importance of place that Wordsworth gives to these vividly recalled games among the influences that were to make him into a poet. He captures, first of all, the illusion of timelessness which happy children enjoy by phrases like 'week to week . . . month to month . . . round of tumult'. Daylight is succeeded by 'twinkling stars', and all the grown-ups who had earlier sat round on benches and doorsteps are asleep, but it is only physical exhaustion which finally drives the children home to bed. Another strong impression is of community: the village square with its central rock is described as 'the goal / Or centre of these sports', and there is the evocative phrase 'A later lingerer' for the old man who watches them longest, as though he is reluctant to depart from this image of his own boyhood. Why does the old man stay last? The suggestion is that youth and age have a sympathy, as in William Blake's 'Echoing Green' (1789), where the old folk all say:

> Such, such were the joys
> When we all, girls and boys
> In our youth time were seen
> On the Echoing Green.

The juxtaposition in this paragraph of the vivid and detailed picture of the past with Wordsworth's present dilemma, of his longing for a 'Union that cannot be', i.e. of adult self-awareness and boyhood spontaneity, is typical of the poem's indifference to chronology. The pattern is repeated when he moves abruptly from the description of the rock as it was in the past to the present scene. The rock has been 'split and gone to build' (1805 version). The new Assembly-room and Wordsworth's verbs show his sense of outrage: 'usurped . . . scream'. Clearly the kind of assembly here is a poor exchange for the total community of his boyhood games, since it is enclosed, out of harmony with the place and presumably divisive (no children or old men). Besides it is destructive of memory of the past, for the stone had been named after the old woman. Yet something is retained: Wordsworth believes that his friends, now men, who will happily dance to the fiddle in this obnoxious room will join him in remembering both the old dame and the 'soft starry nights'. Thus memory both of community and of Nature will work its magic of recall.

II.47–54, 54–78

The energetic pastimes of Wordsworth's boyhood begin to have an added quality. Unless they are connected with the delights of the natural world, they cease to give much pleasure; the example offered is of rowing excursions on Lake Windermere. The first eight lines seem to move from boyhood into adolescence. The 'boisterous course' recalls the 'round of tumult' of earlier games, and again there is the sense of timelessness in 'the year span round'. The second sentence balances this with 'regular . . . calmer' and with the increased self-awareness suggested by 'scheme of holiday delight'. Wordsworth and his friends no longer value mere animal spirits: though they race, they do not mind who wins, and the phrase 'languidly pursued' suggests they are searching for a super-added excitement. This seems to be linked with the imagination, for all the details of the islands they visit show imagination working upon natural beauty to produce a near magical effect; on one island the birds sing ceaselessly, the next is covered with lilies, and on the third there is a ruined shrine which evokes the vision of a romantically religious past. These islands, like the one described later (167–72), are presented to the reader as a real landscape, but they are both real and more than real. Islands have always been a potent image of magic isolation and, though Wordsworth does not emphasise any symbolism here, the detail of the islands does suggest the three religious aspects of communal praise, simplicity and dedication. It is the influence of these islands which both satisfies them all and banishes the usual stresses of everyday life; 'conquered and conqueror' are united, 'uneasiness . . . pain . . . jealousy . . . vain-glory' are 'tempered', so that for the whole group, Nature becomes a moral teacher. Quite suddenly Wordsworth turns from the plural 'we' and 'our' of the rest of the paragraph and speaks directly to Coleridge, linking these idyllic past experiences with his abiding love of solitude. There is a suggestion in the last two lines that his friend has seen some danger in this and that Wordsworth is requiring his sympathetic understanding by relating it to his past.

II.78–114

Food and money were very short in Wordsworth's schooldays. After the twice-a-year holiday, however, he and his brother Christopher would return with just enough money to afford some treats. They bought food from sources other than the old woman who kept the stall by the rock, and had picnics. Sometimes, more extravagantly, they hired horses and went on longer expeditions, though they did not tell the innkeeper just how far they planned to take his horses, perhaps twenty miles to Furness Abbey. While they explored the ruins, the horses grazed and the sea wind from the west passed overhead, the place itself was so sheltered that the trees were as motionless as the ruined abbey towers.

The passage opens with the familiar pendulum movement between Wordsworth old and Wordsworth young. He writes about their privation as schoolboys with mock solemnity, using phrases like 'delicate viands' and 'weekly stipend', suggesting that their upbringing was in the best tradition of classical simplicity and that their hunger increased their strength. Of course, the boys did not see it that way, and Wordsworth passes on to the joy of having money to supply 'treats' and describing pastoral picnics in idyllic settings. He remembers sitting in the shade while the sun 'Unfelt shone brightly round us in our joy'. The negative of the first word echoes the 'unsought' (II.7) power which nature exerted upon him.

The picture here is of the group of boys hugely enjoying their expedition but at the same time being 'sustained' in their joy without realising it by the unremarked sunshine. The delight in physical movement is rhythmically presented in 'proud to curb / And eager to spur on the galloping steed'. This delight will be reiterated in the next paragraph, but it first frames an image of intense quietude – the ancient abbey, the peacefully grazing horses and the contrast between the wind overhead and the 'deep shelter' here. Once again there is a suggestion of enchantment, so that the landscape is not only that of Cumberland but of Malory's *Morte D'Arthur* or Spenser's *Faerie Queene*, for in all these 'Excursions far away among the hills' (1805, II.93) there is a strong suggestion of a protective presence – 'safeguard', 'shelter', 'a holy scene' – to make their joy seem always secure.

II.115–37

The return journey starts with a race, but Wordsworth interrupts his account to recall another 'shaping' incident from their visits to

Furness Abbey when, on a showery, gloomy, 'comfortless' day, an unseen wren had sung so sweetly that he felt he could have stayed there for ever. They do not go straight back to Hawkshead but make detours, sometimes at speed and sometimes slowing to breathe the horses. At these moments, or when they are galloping back across the sands (between Rampside and Greenodd) Wordsworth is conscious of a 'still spirit' pervading the world around him.

The passage is full of contrasts. The noise and tumult of the expedition is repeatedly emphasised – the race through the chauntry is 'uncouth'; 'summons', and 'whip and spur' are in strong contrast to the stillness and silence of the old church and the stone figures on the tombs. Apart from a few details, the abbey is not pictorially described, but the atmosphere of the place is vividly conveyed. There are two emphatic negatives – 'roofless . . . comfortless' – and the faint noises suggesting grief, 'sobbing', 'shuddering', give it a mysterious life. So it is hardly surprising that the boys react as they do: they 'flew' through the walls and 'scampered homewards'. But the song of the unseen wren has a quite different effect: it transforms the rain-soaked ruin into a place where Wordsworth would have liked to stay for ever. Here, therefore, as so often in Wordsworth, there is the fostering 'alike by beauty and by fear' (I.302).

Time, too, is constantly changing: the opening lines establish a specific moment – the remounting and the signal for the party to set off at a gallop – but no sooner have they done so than Wordsworth recalls the song of the wren and then retreats further into time with his description of how 'comfortless' the day had seemed before this song. The movement of Wordsworth's memory is like a winding river: he sets off only to be deflected by a further recollection which will in turn be interrupted. The complex structure of the long first sentence itself reflects the complexity of memory.

II.138–97

Another place visited was an inn on the shores of Lake Windermere. Partly because a great house, Belle Isle, had recently been built nearby, the local inn had been refurbished, and instead of the old, simple cottage with 'one bright fire' and a tree outside for shade in summer, it became a fashionable resort with a constant flow of visitors in coaches. A gaudy new sign with golden letters had replaced the old picture of a lion once painted by a local man. Yet in spite of its glossy modernisation, Wordsworth still loves the place because of the happy times there as schoolboys, playing bowls, feasting and then rowing out at dusk to an island to listen to their flute-player.

This description is the last one in the book of shared schoolboy pleasures, and it is fascinating in several ways. Did the other guests at this superior inn not mind this rowdy group on the bowling green 'making the mountains ring'? And the sophistication of their evening pleasures is striking: they listen in rapt silence to their friend playing, but take care to increase their pleasure by listening to it across the still, shadowy water. They must have been an interesting group: we know that Robert Greenwood, 't'lad wi't flute' as Wordsworth's landlady called him, later became Senior Fellow at Trinity College, Cambridge. Wordsworth's reaction to the modernised inn is a double one, recognising both the delight he had as a boy in its strawberry teas and its splendidly placed bowling green, from which they looked down through tree tops to the lake beneath, but as an adult condemning what it is and what it had destroyed. As so often, his detail assumes metaphorical importance. The door of the inn is 'beset with chaises, grooms, and liveries': the first word suggests threat, and the three nouns imply a world of fashionable luxury threatening the innocence and peace of the 'homely-featured' cottages around. The 'slight and mockery' with which the work of the old local painter had been thrown away is like the unthinking destruction of the old market stone; 'usurped', like 'beset', suggests warfare, and the new sign-board is 'spangled', a contemptuous word.

As in the Furness Abbey passage, noise, physical energy and excitement are succeeded by intense calm: it is this combination which seems to generate Wordsworth's awareness of a special power. In this instance his sensation is that the still evening water and the lovely sky actually pervade his being: they 'lay upon my mind . . . sank down into my heart . . . held me like a dream'. The intensity of his delight triggers the usual sideways movement, and he leaves the description of the evening excursion to recall how he had always loved the sun, distinguished between his rational adult feelings which recognise its 'bounty to so many worlds' and his 'thoughtless' boyhood reaction, when the beauty of the sun and moon gave him instinctive joy. It is from these strange moments of intimacy with the world around him that Wordsworth traces the growth of his love, his 'enlarged sympathy' with all created things, and his three times repeated 'love' (178–9) has something of the insistence of a creed. He speaks of the two most solemn moments of the day, sunrise and sunset, but not with awe. Instead there is a loving gentleness in the way the sun 'lay / His beauty on the morning hills' and the mutual touch in return of the mountains at sunset.

II.198–232

Looking back on adolescence, Wordsworth recognises the definite change between his first love of Nature as the background to all his pleasures – 'the incidental charms' – and the time when he came to love her 'for her own sake'. But he no sooner draws this distinction than he rebels against the idea that such intellectual/spiritual development can be charted exactly. He uses three images only to reject them all. The first is of a mathematical intellect, like that supposed by the philosophers Descartes and Berkeley, and Wordsworth's phraseology – 'parcel out . . . geometric . . . split . . . into round and square' immediately signals his contempt for such a mechanistic approach. The second image is quite different, for here he appeals to the reader, challenging him to identify how the seeds of his own character were sown. Again the impossibility of being exact does not even require a negative. The third image is his favourite one of the human mind as a river, contrasting its fluidity with the precise way a lecturer points out a fact on a blackboard (see also Section 5.3). Now Wordsworth turns tor support to Coleridge, who recognises that knowledge (science) is only a means of expressing ideas, not a guide to the problem. Coleridge is not the kind of thinker who works out a theory and then believes that his own categories are real ones instead of a possible assistance to understanding. He, like Wordsworth, has had the intuition of unity in the universe and therefore doubts all the theorists who are confident that they can class human 'faculties' like specimens in a glass case. Analysis of the mind is difficult or perhaps impossible, for it can be logically argued (231) that the source of every line of thought extends back before the life of the thinker. So, in the next paragraph, Wordsworth will turn to consider the mysterious way in which the 'infant Babe' learns from its mother.

II.232–65

The previous paragraph has called on Coleridge to support Wordsworth's claim that exact rational analysis of the human mind is impossible. Here Wordsworth turns away from an intellectual to an imaginative approach. He meditates upon the close relationship between a new-born baby and its mother where, by every operation of the senses ('Nursed . . . Rocked') and of feelings (237), the child is drawn as by 'gravitation' into the stream of life. This intimate operation demonstrates both literally and symbolically the interaction between 'one great Mind' (257) and the created 'Being' (252). Though the new-born child may seem 'frail . . . outcast . . . bewildered and oppressed', this is not so. The 'dear Presence' of the mother irradiates and exalts every object with tenderness – 'shades of pity'. So when the child encounters external nature – Wordsworth instances a flower – this has a super-added beauty learnt from its mother's love, and it is this feeling which makes it truly human, marks it as an 'inmate of this active universe'. By means of these two interacting forces, its mother's love and external nature, the child can become a 'creator and receiver': that is, it is not merely passive, but by acquiring its ability to work 'in alliance' with experience, it becomes like an 'agent' of the creator. This ability to create a relationship with the external world is, Wordsworth says, the true 'poetic spirit'. The inhibitions which come with growing up (262) weaken or destroy this power for many people, but for some, whatever happens, whether good or bad (264), it remains their most 'pre-eminent' quality.

The pattern of the mother/child relationship is thus worked out on many levels. It is strongly established in its physical sense of warmth, protection, sleeping, feeding. It is linked with the development of sympathetic emotion by which the child can then establish its bonding with all external nature. It is also seen as the genesis for the working of the imagination, which is poetic genius.

The 1805 version of this paragraph has an extra ten lines, and the 1850 version shows much revision, tending to diminish the inborn power of the child. One element omitted in 1850 is Wordsworth's clear statement of the way the child's feelings act as a unifying agent between things that otherwise would be 'loth to coalesce' (1805, II.249). He replaced this with the softer, less challenging and possibly sentimentalised picture of the flower (245–8). He also replaced the earlier identification of the child '*as* an agent of the great mind' with a more tentative comparative, '*like* an agent'.

II.265–322

It was by physical means ('touch') that Wordsworth as a baby had communicated with his mother, and in the language of feeling that he had learnt in this way, Nature continued to educate him during his boyhood as he has described so far in the poem. Now, however, he feels that his difficulties in transforming the 'shadowy ground' of his past into words are going to be more formidable. He picks up from the beginning of the poem the image of a journey, and in 272–5 he gives his path 'broken windings', the dangers of great height ('eagle's wing'), and the need for the skill and strength of a chamois. He claims the reader's help on this difficult ascent with the 'we' of 274, and warns of a new trouble which he did not then understand. The paragraph after 281 will proceed to explore Wordsworth's change of heart more openly, but first he sets his problem in two brief sentences. The first of these repeats from 198–202 the difficulty of describing the change, when his earlier delight in boisterous pleasures acted out against the background of the natural world dwindled away, leaving him instead with a delight in nature itself which would operate even without any 'form or image' (305–6) to inspire it. The second sentence is more ambiguous: it can be read as a metaphorical restatement of Wordsworth's growing independence of sensuous experience, but it can also apply to the death of both his parents, 'the props of my affections'. Both interpretations are justifiable.

Now Wordsworth goes on to record his sharpened sensibility to 'all that I beheld'. This 'finer', 'more exact' observation brought 'knowledge', a word emphatically repeated in 287, where it is linked with 'delight'. Obviously this kind of knowledge has nothing to do with Hawkshead Grammar School, and in typical fashion Wordsworth goes on to clarify his meaning by example. His new awareness makes him notice every tiny detail of the changing seasons which he stores up in the 'register of his memory', and in the next eight lines (294–301) he lists the beneficent results of this accumulated knowledge. Of these, the one that is most clearly stated is his pleasure in solitude, since in this state he becomes particularly aware of what he calls 'concords' or 'permanent relations'. Perhaps the easiest way to understand how important to Wordsworth is this perception of likeness in the superficially unlike, is to think of the immense insight that can come to us from reading a brilliantly conceived simile or metaphor. So Wordsworth's understanding of 'life, and change, and beauty' (294) is enlarged by this new 'watchful power'.

Wordsworth then offers a more circumstantial example, although it is typical of the increasing asceticism of his communion with the world around him that his 'visionary power' now comes to him in a night made even darker 'with a coming storm', as he listens to the mysterious 'language of the ancient earth', manifested in the sounds of water and of the wind. Wordsworth started this paragraph by recalling the primitive language of touch between baby and mother; he next explored the way that meticulous use of sight could feed spiritual understanding; now he listens, in the dark, to strange non-human sounds, and since he says these are 'unprofaned' by images – verbal? visual? both? – they presumably lead him ever closer to the heart of his experience.

Finally, the combination of sensuous and spiritual in his image 'drink the visionary power' (which can remind us of the much younger Wordsworth of I.578–81) returns us to the central problem of the paragraph, the difficulty of finding language which will convey these 'fleeting' experiences. The soul remembers 'how she felt, but what she felt / Remembering not'. Paradoxically, however, the memory recalls such visitations with increased desire to 'pursue', and with the last two lines of the paragraph we are back with the image of the mountain path and the irresistible urge to go yet higher, i.e. the poet's need to explore and to communicate his subject.

II.323–52

This deep communion with nature came in calm weather as well as in the 'night blackened with a coming storm' of the previous paragraph. Now Wordsworth recollects how he used to wander round 'our little lake', Esthwaite Water, with John Fleming, his dear friend of that time. School at Hawkshead began at about 6.30 a.m. in summer and an hour later in winter, so these walks must indeed have been 'early'. Sometimes he would go out even earlier and alone, so that by the time dawn broke and the thrush began to sing, young Wordsworth would have climbed up to some high point from where he could look down on the totally deserted valley. So powerful was the effect of this solitude upon him that the actual landscape ('prospect') seemed to become an interior vision, and 'bodily eyes were utterly forgotten'.

The larger patterning of the poem, the subtle interconnection of paragraphs, is well exemplified here: the last held a description of walking by starlight in storm; now it is fair weather and dawn. The half-line that starts this paragraph has 'And not alone', this being poised almost exactly between the 'walk alone' of 302 and the 'alone' of 344. The memory of John Fleming is given special poignancy because they have lost touch: 'our minds / Both silent to each other'. What is the effect of this sudden recollection of a beloved friend? Partly it exemplifies the powerful operation of memory: although *now* there is no special relationship between them (338), the emotion of the past, connected as it is with those Esthwaite walks, remains as valid as ever and, Wordsworth believes, memory would work as strongly upon his friend (334–5). As the reiterated 'alone' suggests, the poet summons up this happy relationship only to demonstrate that the 'latent power' he was discovering around him was so strong that he needed no human companionship for it to operate upon him. The concluding lines, where his actual sight of the valley is transformed into a visionary experience, recalls the description of the evening party upon Windermere where they listened to the flute-player over the still water. There, too, Wordsworth says, he was held 'like a dream' (174).

As always, Wordsworth is restless under the difficulties of recounting these experiences in words – a difficulty always encountered by writers attempting to define mystical experience. Sometimes there is a religious tone as in 'holy calm', the terminology of philosophy with 324–6, and towards the end of the paragraph the despairing questions: 'How . . . where . . . ?'

II.352–76

Every season, every time of day, sleeping or waking, feeds Wordsworth's 'religious' communion with Nature. The list tumbles out like a cornucopia of riches: 'inexhaustible', he says, and 'poured forth'. All the more abrupt, then, is the monosyllabic emphasis which starts the second sentence: 'But let this be not forgotten'. What Wordsworth is so unequivocally reminding his reader of is man's own unique capability in the face of this avalanche of experience – his 'creative sensibility', 'plastic power' – and this by no means always conforms obediently to the promptings of the 'regular actings of the world', a phrase which seems to link with the cycle of seasons and times of day in the opening lines. This rebellion, 'devious mood', 'war', then gives way to a 'subservience'. A poet's ability to create develops from such tension, and it is exactly this tension which he described at the beginning of the poem (I.35–8).

When his creative power is running in tandem with the nature around him, then it enriches it with added power and splendour: his mind provides an 'auxiliar' light: that is, he claims for his poetic power a similar gift to God's creation of light. It is because Nature so fuels this power that he pays it joyful worship: 'my obeisance, my devotion'.

II.376–418

The book is working towards the triumphant lyric climax which will follow line 400, but first there is a recall, a summary of Wordsworth's understanding of himself, his gifts and the Nature that has formed him. His distrust of rational analysis remembers lines 228 and 203; his faith that his inspiration is based on the perception of a unity where others might only see differences is that of 297–300. Now, looking back on his blissful seventeen-year-old self, he offers alternative explanations. The first is that he had projected his own intense feelings on to the world around, thus giving 'unorganic natures' a sympathetic life which might not be really there, and that this 'habit' was so deeply engrained in him that he was unaware of it. The second possibility is that he did receive a revelation from an actual force, that he did 'converse with things that really are'. But Wordsworth has already said that it is 'vain hope, to analyse the mind' and he leaves the 'whether . . . or . . . or' rationally open, moving instead into such a triumphant paean of praise to the reality of his communion with a force beyond himself, that the question is implicitly answered.

The recurring image in this hymn of wonder is that of water: 'Blessings spread around me like a sea', he says, and the idea of moving water is repeated in 'Nature overflowing'. His thought is 'steeped in feeling', and when he has enumerated the manifestations of life of which he feels part – 'all that leaps and runs and shouts and sings / Or beats the gladsome air' – he returns for his climactic image to everything living in the sea, in the movement of the waves and in the profundity of the water. The language here is full of echoes of that version of the Bible which Wordsworth would have heard every day at school, both the celebration in the Psalms of the mighty sea and the story of the creation when the spirit moved upon the face of the waters. These are unified for him with Windermere and Esthwaite and all the other beloved lakes, and the sea as he saw it under the rising moon (I.567–80).

However vitally Wordsworth's senses react to this world, as is evidenced by the six strongly physical verbs of 406–7, there is always an even more powerful communication. This is not only out of reach of thought and knowledge (403–4), but neither human eye (404) nor ear (410) can register it. It could be initiated by the 'humblest prelude' of some sensuous experience, but when that was over and the ear, to use Wordsworth's metaphor here, 'slept undisturbed', it was then that this song of joy was 'most audible'. The pattern here is of an awareness leaving intellectual apprehension aside and moving through intense physical awareness into an acute and open sensibility of 'the heart' (405) which brought a communion 'through earth and heaven / With every form of creature'.

Most of this paragraph dates back to February/March 1798, when it was written for a short poem, *The Ruined Cottage*. This makes it contemporary with *Tintern Abbey*, where Wordsworth uses a different image, 'looking into the life of things' for the same experience.

For the change Wordsworth made in this passage to avoid the interpretation that he believed the universe was governed by a pantheistic force, see Section 4.4.

II.419–51

Even if others find a different faith by different means and Wordsworth's interpretation of his spiritual journey is mistaken ('if this be error'), he knows for certain that he owes everything to the countryside which has nurtured him. It is this which has taught him to be 'pure in heart', content with himself, and indifferent to ambition which brings 'little enmities and low desires'. Above all, it has given him courage to retain faith in human nature, even when contemporary events (432) might have produced despair.

This passage is clearly related to the letter which Coleridge sent to Wordsworth in 1799, urging him to write a poem about those 'who, in consequence of the failure of the French Revolution, have thrown up all hope of the amelioration of mankind, and are sinking into epicurean selfishness'. By 1799, the glowing liberal hopes of Liberty, Equality and Fraternity had faded away. The 'good men' (435) had abandoned any faith in political action and returned to private life, amid the 'wicked exultation' of those who had always opposed reform and widespread cynicism about the 'visionary minds', such as those of Wordsworth, Coleridge and their friends who still persisted in believing in the possibility of a better society.

This paragraph starts on a note of apparent uncertainty, only to change swiftly into a triumphant or defiant assertion of faith. The first sentence is organised round two conditional clauses – 'if this be error', 'if I should fail' – but the self-doubt implied here is quietly countered by the way the sentence moves to rest in Wordsworth's grateful salutation of 'mountains . . . lakes . . . cataracts . . . winds'. With the next sentence the tempo increases: it is twenty-one lines long, with the kind of aggressive complexity which – quite properly here – suggests the tone of a passionate political speech. This sentence also starts with 'if' and will repeat this four more times, but these conjunctions are now used not negatively but positively. Each one introduces a further emphatic challenge: if I could survive *this* and *this*, he says, then my faith was 'more than Roman'. The reference feels absolutely right here – 'Roman' suggests a struggle for liberty, endurance and austerity and was indeed the way in which the French republicans saw themselves, as the paintings of David (1748–1825) exactly demonstrate. But Wordsworth speaks of his 'confidence' exceeding this, for his 'support . . . fails not', whatever the 'dereliction and dismay' that besets the failure of political hopes. At this point the sentence reaches its triumphant climax, with a restatement of Wordsworth's creed: again he hails 'winds . . . cataracts . . . mountains', but now with a threefold exclamation. (For further comment see Section 5.3.)

The last sentence provides a coda. For the third time in this paragraph, Wordsworth salutes his source of understanding and of joy, enclosing within the sentence his belief why such strength is necessary – to sustain 'this uneasy heart of ours'.

II.451–66, 466–70

Book II starts with a direct address to Coleridge, companion and adviser on his journey into the past, and it ends with a farewell. Late in 1799, when the first version of this passage was written, Coleridge had left the Lakes for the life of a journalist in London. Wordsworth recalls how different their upbringings had been, and the phrase 'reared in the great city' is a quotation from Coleridge's poem *Frost at Midnight*, written only a year before. Coleridge has spent his boyhood at school in London, in Christ's Hospital, while Wordsworth had all the freedom of Hawkshead. Yet, Wordsworth claims, they had reached the same 'bourne' – they had come to share the same philosophy. Both relied upon the insight brought by solitary communion with Nature, and the final lines envisage Coleridge still drawing his 'heathful mind' from solitude, even when he is in the 'haunts of men'.

It is in the central sentence that Wordsworth describes just what the companionship of Coleridge meant to him, for in him he had found rare sympathetic understanding both of his beliefs and his writing. This helped him to survive the contemptuous criticism of his work, both explicit (456) and implicit (457–60). How deeply felt this mockery was is shown by the way his mind reverts to it. A passage in

Lines written above Tintern Abbey (128–30) carries the same message – 'the sneers of selfish men . . . greetings where no kindness is' – and in all the revisionary years between 1799 and 1850, this passage stands virtually unchanged. It is sad to realise how this heartfelt acknowledgement of friendship – 'In many things my brother' – contrasts with the rift of later years. However, in all the subsequent revisions of the poem, Wordsworth allowed no hint of estrangement to cloud his original gratitude.

3 WORDSWORTH IN CONTEXT

3.1 WORDSWORTH AND THE FRENCH REVOLUTION

The first half of Wordsworth's life was a period of widespread and profound political instability. In 1776, when he was six years old, the North American colonies decided that they and their forefathers had not emigrated from England to go on enduring what they saw as fiscal and political oppression, and decided to seize the freedom they desired by force. It is hard now to imagine the astonished dismay in England when the American states tore themselves away from the mother-country, and the even greater sense of disbelief when their revolution succeeded. France had been quick to give military aid to help America to freedom but very soon found that the intoxicating ideas of liberty, equality and fraternity were just as attractive to Frenchmen. By 1789 revolution had started in France, marked by the violent capture and destruction of the Bastille, the fortress-like prison which symbolised a tyrannical regime. It was exactly a year after the fall of the Bastille that the twenty-year-old Wordsworth arrived in Calais with his friend Jones for a three-month walking holiday. Everywhere they were welcomed into the dancing and feasting in the streets, 'bright with happy faces and with garlands hung' that celebrated this anniversary. There was widespread confidence in England as well as in France that reform would now proceed peacefully and constitutionally towards a just society: as Wordsworth later sadly recorded,

> Europe at that time was thrilled with joy,
> France standing on the top of golden hours,
> And human nature seeming born again (VI.339.41).

But the revolution, as revolutions do, became increasingly violent as the struggle for power intensified. Wordsworth, innocent of the impending storm, decided when he left Cambridge the next year that he would return to France to perfect his French. He was to remain there just a year, and this year marked him permanently, as he describes in the tenth book of *The Prelude*. On his arrival he was interested in public events but was personally uninvolved and politically quite unsophisticated. With obvious self-derision he compares his ignorance of the realities of political life to that of a sheltered plant in a greenhouse – 'a parlour shrub / That spreads its leaves in unmolested peace / While every bush and tree the country through, / Is shaking to the roots'; he had 'abruptly passed / Into a theatre, whose stage was filled / And busy with an action far advanced' (IX.88–95). A year later all this was changed, not only because of political events but because of their interaction with two people. He was deeply influenced by a remarkable man, Captain Michel Beaupuy, a soldier some six years his senior who had thrown in his lot with the forces of the revolution. He also fell passionately in love with Annette Vallon, who in December 1792 bore him a daughter, Caroline.

To the second of these events Wordsworth makes no direct reference in *The Prelude*. The 1805 version does include a tale of two lovers, Vaudracour and Julia, which can be interpreted as a version of his own story, but even this was later detached from the autobiographical context of the poem and published independently in 1820. After Wordsworth's death his family decided to omit any reference to the affair in the official memoir, and not until this century did the sad little story emerge. It is probable that Wordsworth slipped back to Paris secretly at the height of the Terror in October 1793, but if so, he did not reach Annette, and war between France and England meant he could not see her again for the next ten years until the brief Peace of Amiens. Even letters rarely got through: two of Annette's to William, stopped by the censor, remained undiscovered in French archives until 1923. The misery of this enforced parting, the guilt and self-blame which Wordsworth undoubtedly suffered, made worse by the need for secrecy, become yet another formative influence on *The Prelude*.

About Michel Beaupuy, Wordsworth is as communicative as he is silent about Annette. Soon after their meeting in Orléans, they become close friends, endlessly discussing social injustice, the causes of poverty and the urgent need for change. Beaupuy seems to have been an unusual man, highly principled yet tolerant, humane and idealistic, but with no illusions about the stupidity and violence which poverty fosters and which would inevitably disfigure revolutionary action. From him Wordsworth felt he learned the most important lessons in life, a shared sense of humanity with all men, a social conscience which made him see poverty not as a necessary condition for some, but as an evil to be righted, and to look with indignant horror on social inequalities of privileged wealth and birth, and the pretence, pomposity and self-consequence they bred. All this is summed up in a moving episode described by Wordsworth. On one of their many walks they met a 'hunger-bitten girl' whose listless misery so stirs Beaupuy that he 'In agitation said, "Tis against that / That we

are fighting" ', and Wordsworth is filled with hope that soon
we should see the earth

> Unthwarted in her wish to recompense
> The meek, the lowly, patient child of toil.
> All institutes for ever blotted out
> That legalised exclusion, empty pomp abolished . . .

Wordsworth only knew Beaupuy for four months: he died in action in
1796 fighting the Austrians. Before that Wordsworth, under the
influence of William Godwin's *Political Justice*, had changed his mind
about active revolution, but the generous agitation which Beaupuy,
'my patriot friend', had communicated to his receptive young companion never left him. The imaginative sympathy which he extended to
solitaries, the poor and the unhappy, as well as his invincible belief in
'man and his noble nature' owed a great deal to Beaupuy.

On his way home in October 1792, Wordsworth lingered for six
weeks in Paris, as we know from *The Prelude*. The city was in a
ferment of political unrest, volatile and dangerous, 'a place of
fear . . . Defenceless as a wood where tigers roam'. The previous
month had seen the massacre of about eight thousand prisoners, the
royal family were in prison, the guillotine dominated the Place du
Carrousel, a Prussian army was invading France's borders, and a
murderous struggle for power was going on between the Jacobin
extremists, with Robespierre, Danton and Marat at their head, and
the more moderate Girondins led by Brissot. Wordsworth once told
his nephew that he was 'intimately connected' with this latter party,
as was his companion at that time, James Watt, son of the famous
engineer. Robespierre actually issued an order for the latter's arrest
and young James had to flee from Paris. The same could easily have
happened to Wordsworth, or that more terrible fate which befell the
Girondin leaders a little later when they were sent to the guillotine.
Wordsworth testified to this possibility when he wrote, twelve years
after this tumultuous period,

> Doubtless I should have then made common cause
> With some who perished; haply, perished too,
> A poor mistaken and bewildered offering,-
> Should to the breast of Nature have gone back,
> With all my resolutions, all my hopes,
> A Poet only to myself, to men
> Useless . . .

In fact, Wordsworth was to be preserved by a most humdrum
consideration: a total absence of money. His guardians rightly felt
that Paris was the last place in which to be loitering and cut off
supplies. Wordsworth therefore had no option but to leave the
'hurricane' of political events in Paris, unwillingly abandon Annette

in Blois a few weeks before she was to bear their child, and return 'of harsh necessity' to England. He would not find political peace of mind there either.

3.2   THE 'CALAMITOUS SITUATION' IN ENGLAND

Wordsworth had always felt himself a natural democrat, a fellow countryman of Milton. The society in which he was born and bred, and the austere Protestantism which taught every human being his inviolable responsibility for his own actions, naturally fostered that independence of mind which accepts no authority but that of conscience. In *The Prelude* Wordsworth congratulates himself upon his great good fortune in being 'born in a poor district . . . of ancient homeliness', where

> It was my fortune scarcely to have seen,
> Through the whole tenor of my school-day time,
> The face of one, who, whether boy or man,
> Was vested with attention or respect
> Through claims of wealth or blood (IX.218–22)

What is more, both his school and Cambridge University offered him, he rather surprisingly claims, the example 'of a republic . . . they were brothers all'. So it is easy to see how Beaupuy's political teaching of liberty, equality and fraternity spoke to a mind well prepared to recognise it as not only eminently rational but natural and morally right. What, however, seems to have come as a great shock to the politically ingenuous young Wordsworth was the growing realisation that the general situation in his own country was very different from the Cumberland and Cambridge in which he had grown up.

Certainly on his return to England in 1792, Wordsworth was both astonished and dismayed by the militaristic jingoism that pervaded his 'beloved country'. England had become the ally of the old tyrannical powers of Austria and Prussia and declared war on France, an act he regarded as not only against her true interests but as evidence that 'even thinking minds / Forgot that such a sound was ever heard / As liberty . . . ' While England was engaged in a war which Wordsworth at first thought unjustifiable, and which was certainly markedly unsuccessful, the news from France was equally horrifying to the lover of liberty. The Jacobins were jealously guarding their power by widespread executions without trial – the Great Terror as it came to be called – and Wordsworth found himself afflicted by nightmares when he was 'entangled . . . in long orations, which I strove to plead / Before unjust tribunals' (X.410–12). The downfall of Robespierre in 1794 brought him intense relief: 'few happier moments have been mine', but then France herself embarked upon wars of imperial aggression which threw up the figure, monstrous in Wordsworth's eyes, of Napoleon.

England, however, seemed just as ready to resort to injustice and legalised tyranny, and a series of repressive acts between 1792 and 1798 took away the rights of public meeting, of free speech and of the free press. 1795 was a particularly unhappy year: there had been two bad harvests and industry was suffering because of the war. The realisation that there was now no hope of constitutional reform led to angry demonstrations, and the King's state coach had its windows shattered on his way to open Parliament. Inevitably fear inspired further repression, and the country became flooded with government spies and informers. In 1794 the Bishop of Llandaff published a sermon praising God's wisdom in creating poor as well as rich. Wordsworth's fury broke out in a political pamphlet. He attacked, among other topics, the monarchy, any absolute constitution, the absurdity of social grandeur and pomp, the 'thorny labyrinth' of litigation, the injustice of a society which produced poverty and so endangered marriage, and imperialist wars which increased the misery of the poor. Not surprisingly it was not published: William's lawyer brother, Richard, warned him that the very mention of politics could land him in prison. The *Habeas Corpus* Act, which prevented people being imprisoned on mere suspicion, or without trial, had been suspended, and no publisher could take the risk, but the pamphlet provides an invaluable insight into Wordsworth's state of mind at this time.

The atmosphere of danger and suspicion was widespread and Richard's warnings were shown to be prudent: when the Coleridges and Wordsworths were at Alfoxden in 1797, they were kept under surveillance by a singularly inept government spy called Walsh, and as late as 1808, Wordsworth was gloomily convinced he might be sent to Newgate Prison.

In fact, by the time they were at Alfoxden, with reports on the group's activities being carefully filed at the Home Office, Wordsworth was responding to the benign influence of Dorothy and the stimulation of Coleridge, to come to terms with the sad aftermath of the French Revolution and the collapse of all his political hopes. He would never again have any confidence in political action, but the extraordinary experiences of his time in France, unshared by any contemporary writer, were ready to be directed into a completely different enterprise. In 1799, Coleridge wrote to Wordsworth: 'I wish you would write a poem in blank verse, addressed to those, who, in consequence of the complete failure of the French Revolution, have thrown up all hopes of the amelioration of mankind and are sinking into almost epicurean selfishness.' Wordsworth had already embarked upon just such a poem. He would retrack his life to find exactly how the experiences of his twenty-nine years had formed him into the being that he was and offer to his reader his own sources of strength from the Nature that had formed him.

It is only by assimilating the political context in which Wordsworth wrote that the reader can give proper understanding to the turbulence, the 'unmanageable thoughts', which gave urgency to his need to write *The Prelude*.

3.3 THE ROMANTIC MOVEMENT

The political upheavals in America and Europe were paralleled by a development of ideas later to be called the Romantic Movement, but while Wordsworth, Blake, Coleridge, Byron, Shelley and Keats are all categorised as Romantic poets, there has been much argument about the meaning of the term. We can at least assume that it is centrally involved with the importance of individualism and a rejection of authority in all its manifestations. From this comes the challenging of the authority of the state, particularly in the form of any oligarchy or hereditary monarchy and anger at infringements of personal liberty by those in power. Bound up with this is a contempt for all manifestations of social superiority, of class distinction based on possessions or on family. The Church's ancient claims to authority were equally denied: the Romantic would allow no organisation to dictate to him what he ought to believe or, indeed, what he ought to do. It was the responsibility of each individual soul to work out his own salvation, to establish his own creed and his own moral code. The supremacy of reason associated with the Enlightenment of the eighteenth century was also regarded with the deepest suspicion. Ever since the great seventeenth-century scientist, Isaac Newton, had demonstrated that it was possible to measure the universe, science had been held in awe, and the intelligent eighteenth-century European had generally believed that it was only a matter of time before a similar exact knowledge would be extended to all terrestrial manifestations of nature. This would, of course, include the workings of the mind of man himself – and the thought of such invasion of his soul filled the Romantic with a feeling of revulsion. To an age now familiar with the idea of brain-washing such reaction can seem very justifiable.

Since the Romantic refused the maps offered by traditional political, theological and intellectual authorities, how was he to discover what he was and what he ought to do? In this exploration, the Romantic artist, since he possessed to a greater degree than other men the qualities of creative imagination and a 'sensibility both deep and quick' (Coleridge), assumed a special, almost heroic status. He might seek the answer to his questions in the mediaeval or legendary past, through drink or dreams, sometimes drug-induced. He might find illumination from communion with innocents, such as children, solitaries or outcasts; in sexual or political adventure; but above all by means of the lonely pilgrimage and by a surrender to the power of the natural world, in its remoter and wilder aspects.

The genesis of this movement is impossible to date precisely, but by the late eighteenth century it was strongly established in Germany, France and England, the swift cross-fertilisation of ideas being accelerated by remarkable writers like Rousseau and Goethe (see Section 4). Like them, Wordsworth fits the pattern offered to him by the needs of his time. We can understand why William Hazlitt saw him as 'carried along by the revolutionary movement of his age', but of course Hazlitt had not read *The Prelude* and we can see it goes deeper than that. First there is his intense, visionary sympathy with the countryside of his birth, which was much more powerful for him than any conventional religion. Then there is his conviction that it is the 'winds and sounding cataracts' that have supplied his true education. There is his interest from very early years in solitary figures. There is his eager political enthusiasm for establishing a just society and his passion for liberty, and when these hopes are extinguished, he naturally turns to the next Romantic solution: a pilgrimage into his own individual past, with the Romantic hope that he would thus be able to rescue his fellow-men from their state of 'almost savage torpor' and guide them to a fulfilled life.

The Romantic was innovator and rebel in form as well as content, and the manifesto of Wordsworth's 'revolutionary experiments', as he called them, is clearly stated in the 1800 Preface to the *Lyrical Ballads*, as well as being exemplified in the ballads themselves. Wordsworth's revolt was against the 'gaudy and inane phraseology' which he believed had corrupted poetry for the previous century. Most writers of that period would have agreed that language was the dress of thought and that this dress, to attract an audience, needed to be ornamented with figures of speech: 'True wit is nature to advantage dressed, / What oft was thought, but ne'er so well expressed', said Alexander Pope in 1711. To the Romantic poet, this idea was morally wrong, since Nature demanded sincerity, spontaneity and immediate fusion between thought and feeling. Of course, the language of poets would use figures of speech since language is of its very nature metaphorical, but the images must be born out of the poet's own experience, not plucked casually out of the fashionable literary language of the time. The bareness of diction in Wordsworth's ballads demonstrates the strength of his reaction against his predecessors: in *The Prelude*, this aggressive bareness has developed into the sinewy, cunning simplicity of his evocation of the past on which the authority of the poem depends.

3.4 SCIENCE: WORDSWORTH AND SIR HUMPHREY DAVY

The dividing line between science and art has become so rigid over the last hundred years that we need to remember how differently the world was seen when Wordsworth was a young man. In particular, if we are to recognise what he was attempting to do in *The Prelude* we must be prepared to view it as a scientific exploration, when the tabulation of phenomena (his formative experiences) are then exhaustively considered in the light of a possible theory (the unifying power of nature). The critic M. H. Abrams said of Wordsworth that he was an 'honest heir to the centuries-old tradition of empiricism', and the fact that the Romantics looked with distrust upon the activities of scientists does not mean that they despised scientific reason and method, but that they were convinced there were also other, equally powerful means of discovery. Wordsworth's admiration for Newton, his love of mathematics, his habit of close and prolonged observation of natural and psychological events and that strange dream which records the only things worth rescuing from cataclysm as poetry and science, all help us to see him in proper perspective and to explain, for instance, the considerable effect he had on a man like Charles Darwin.

By the end of the eighteenth century, the study of nature was regarded as the obvious occupation of all intelligent people, although their personal gifts would indicate different approaches. Dr Johnson, the lexicographer, and Edward Gibbon, the classical historian, both became fascinated by chemistry. The friendship between Wordsworth and the greatest British chemist of his day, Humphrey Davy (1778–1829), shows how natural this interaction of interests was still considered to be when Wordsworth, wanting someone he could trust to see the second edition of the *Lyrical Ballads* through the press in 1800, immediately thought of Davy. (Wordsworth was by now in Grasmere and the publisher was in Bristol, where Davy's brilliant career was just beginning.) Wordsworth therefore sent Davy the manuscripts, asking him to correct the punctuation, at which he rather surprisingly admitted he was 'no adept', and to look over the proofs when they were ready. It was the natural choice: Davy much admired Wordsworth's poetry, which he found 'full of just pictures of what human life ought to be'. He himself had written a considerable amount of poetry, such as *The Sacred Stream of Science*, which combines an unashamed and typically Romantic sensibility, a devotion to his scientific vocation, and a deep love of the wild Cornish coast where he was born.

In many ways the background and upbringing of the two was similar, both being born and educated in a remote countryside which they loved, although whereas Wordsworth went to Cambridge and found it unstimulating, Davy was apprenticed to a Penzance surgeon where his freedom to conduct experiments in the attic made him blissfully happy. Both men seem to have possessed great magnetism, both were exceedingly ambitious in their own sphere, and both had a passion for nature which verged on pantheism.

When he was only twenty-three, Davy was appointed director of the chemical laboratory in the newly formed and prestigious Royal Institution for Diffusing Knowledge, in London, and began his seminal work on electro-chemistry, establishing that affinity between chemicals was electrical in nature. What very much marks him, as well as Wordsworth, as a man of his time is the idiosyncrasy of his experimental methods. It must be remembered that scientific methodology was far less rigid at that time – it was in itself necessarily innovative and exploratory. Even so, Davy's methods of discovering the effects of inhaling certain gases were startling, as when he investigated the properties of nitrous oxide (laughing gas) by inhaling sixteen quarts of it himself.

What a comparison of Wordsworth and Davy can do is remind the twentieth-century reader of how similarly the two men would have seen their objectives. They intended to discover, by means of the most determined observation and reflection, more about nature in its every manifestation, and both assumed that their work would be of the greatest utility to the society in which they lived. Davy's poetry, his delight in climbing Helvellyn with Wordsworth and Walter Scott, are an immediate clue to the width of his enthusiasms; what is of equal importance is the way in which the scientific, empirical approach underlies the structure of *The Prelude*.

4 THEMES AND ISSUES

4.1 ROMANTIC 'SELF-BIOGRAPHY'

'Autobiography' is first recorded in English in 1797, so to Wordsworth it would have sounded as unfamiliar as that other recent
invention, 'psychology'. Nevertheless, several popular types of writing can be seen converging to produce the new form which *The
Prelude* exemplifies. Spiritual journals, of which St Augustine's
Confessions was perhaps the first, and John Bunyan's *Grace Abound-
ing*, a popular seventeenth-century version, offer the pattern of
intense interior scrutiny and the alternation of confidence and despair
which are also to be found in Wordsworth. Defoe's use of the
first-person narrator form to disguise his fictions for the Puritan
market produced best-sellers: *Robinson Crusoe*, with its combination
of lively narrative and brooding reflection, was an especial favourite
of young Wordsworth.

In Germany, the type of novel, often semi-autobiographical, which
followed the development of a hero from infancy to maturity was well
established by the time Wordsworth started writing. It was known by
the formidable term *Bildungsroman*, i.e. development-novel. An
English reader can most easily focus the genre by remembering the
mixture of autobiography and imagination in Dickens's *David Cop-
perfield*. The most popular were by the philosopher-poet Goethe.
The Sorrows of Young Werther (1774) set a fashion all over Europe
for soul-searching by young men, and two new words became very
fashionable: *Weltschmerz*, the sense of finding the world an alien
place, and *Ichschmerz*, dissatisfaction with oneself. The reader of
Prelude I will readily recognise how much *Ichschmerz* Wordsworth
has to contend with before he finds his vocation. The most famous
French example of a writer meticulously charting the circumstances
that had made him what he was, were the *Confessions* of Jean-
Jacques Rousseau, written between 1765 and 1770.

The spiritual journal, the innovations of Defoe, the recent fashionable forms of the *Bildungsroman* and the *Confessions*, all contributed

to Wordsworth's understanding of how he could transform the traditional epic into the vehicle he needed.

4.2 THE EDUCATION OF THE CHILD

One of the ways in which Rousseau's admirers believed he had emancipated the human mind was in regard to the education of children. As well as teaching that virtue was linked with the beauty of the natural world and that passion, if sincere, was innocent and good, he held an almost mystic belief in the sacred quality of childhood. In 1762 Rousseau published a treatise on education entitled *Emile*. This demanded respect for children as children instead of treating them as embryo adults. Before this, educational methods had depended on the belief that the child's mind was an empty page upon which teachers should impress ideas in order to fashion a useful member of society. This was anathema to Rousseau, who believed that there was no original sin in the human heart and that vice only entered in through the bungling interference of teachers. The child should be left free to discover reality through experience, and especially through the experience offered by the senses rather than through words. The only book allowed was *Robinson Crusoe*, which Rousseau regarded as an exemplar of learning through experience. This 'charter of youthful deliverance' aroused widespread enthusiasm: in England alone 200 treatises on *Emile* were published before 1800. Rousseau's influence on the way people hereafter thought about children was profound, though the effect on education was often the reverse of what he had intended.

Rousseau's belief in the uniquely intuitive wisdom of the child and the danger of corrupting this by set teaching was shared by Wordsworth. 'The Immortality Ode' (1803) contains the famous vision of the new-born child:

> trailing clouds of glory do we come
> From God, who is our home:
> Heaven lies about us in our infancy.
> Shades of the prison house begin to close
> Upon the growing Boy . . .

Wordsworth's fear of what damage can be done is as acute as Rousseau's. In Book V of *The Prelude* he bitterly attacks 'modern' methods of education, which he accuses of aiming to produce an unnatural and cocksure young adult instead of letting the child learn to respond instinctively to the moral teaching of the world around him.

When Wordsworth looks back on his own early years to understand his present condition, he seems to behold his own upbringing as in the ideally Rousseau-esque tradition. He remembers his childhood primarily in terms of liberty; from this liberty he is able to derive a rich store of sensuous experience which in turn feeds his creative imagination with images of beauty and terror. The modern reader realises the picture he gives is highly selective, but Wordsworth always thought of the poem not as factual autobiography but as describing the growth of his mind. Since his image of himself was essentially that of a poet, what he is trying to discern are only those influences that forged his poetic imagination. These he eventually named with the curious but vivid phrase, 'spots of time'. When he first came to write *The Prelude*, he linked these formative moments only with childhood: 'Such moments chiefly seem to have their date / In our first childhood' (1799, I.295–6). In later versions, Wordsworth recognises that these spots of time could also occur in later life – for instance his experiences in France – but he is still emphatic in placing the 'hiding places of man's power' in what he calls the dawn of life (XII.278–80). In the same paragraph, he acknowledges that as an adult 'I am lost, but see / In simple childhood, something of the base / On which thy greatness stands' ('thy' refers to mankind at its finest). The work of psychologists over the last century has totally familiarised us with the idea that the 'child is father of the man', but Wordsworth's commitment to this belief and his working out of it in terms of his own personality had true originality. It was also to exercise a powerful influence upon subsequent writers. For instance, both Dickens and George Eliot in their finest novels show how their adult heroes and heroines grow inevitably out of the experiences of their childhood. George Eliot makes specific acknowledgement of Wordsworth's lifelong influence upon her. Her belief that only by studying what is growing can we understand the grown, agrees exactly with Wordsworth's interpretation of the organic relationship between child and man.

4.3 WORDSWORTH'S ORIGINALITY IN EPIC AND LANDSCAPE POETRY

Wordsworth's concept of the epic was bound up with ancient ideas of the poet's ability as a gift from the gods. When the bard spoke it was by divine inspiration, so what he said would bring a special illumination to his hearers. They would gain increased understanding of the strange ways of the gods, and of the heroism, cunning or self-sacrifice which men must practise to come to terms with their world and achieve fulfilment. Often the dominant image used is that of a journey, which later became allied to the Christian idea of life as a pilgrimage. So Odysseus, in Homer's epic, has to strive for ten long years to make his way home from Troy; Virgil's Aeneas has similar difficulties before he is able to accomplish his destiny of founding Rome; and Spenser, in the *The Faerie Queene*, recounts the complex search of the Red Cross Knight in his search for true honour. Of all epic poems, however, it was Milton's *Paradise Lost* that was closest to Wordsworth's mind, as the frequent verbal echoes testify. Milton's explicit purpose was to 'justify the ways of God to man' by showing just how and why evil entered the world and Adam and Eve were driven out of Paradise. In the long list of subjects Wordsworth gave in Book I, he was clearly searching for a similarly strong didactic purpose, emerging from a narrative where human dilemmas and spiritual forces interacted. Then came the realisation that the subject of his epic poem had to be his own spiritual journey, including his conquest of doubt concerning his ability as a poet, so that he could pass on his creed to a troubled society that urgently needed the comfort he could give it. He had already said of his shorter poems that they would 'co-operate with the benign tendencies in human nature and society . . . be efficacious in making men wiser, better and happier', and this belief in an inspired task coalesced completely with his concept of the epic.

In the eighteenth century the traditional pastoral, where an idealised picture of rural life was often associated with an allegorical message, had become an exhausted literary form. Instead, poetry with a well-observed country background became popular: James Thomson's *The Seasons* (1730) made his fortune. This alternates meticulously reported landscapes, usually with foreground figures of men and animals with suitable, often pious, comment; John Dyer's *The Fleece* (1757) combines fine descriptions with fascinating information about the wool trade; and John Langhorne's *Country Justice* (1774) was particularly admired by Wordsworth for its observation of agricultural technology, which, he said, 'brought the muse into common life'. Even more he admired William Cowper (1731–1800) because he was 'passionately fond of natural objects'. To read any of these now is to realise how different were Wordsworth's own objectives in *The Prelude*. Perhaps equally revealing is to compare him with a poet whose writing about country life Wordsworth emphatically disliked. George Crabbe's *The Village* (1783) certainly brought the muse into common life, since it painted a grimly convincing picture of rural poverty and degradation in Suffolk. But Wordsworth would not admit this was poetry at all, mere 'verses . . . mere matters of fact, with which the Muses have just about as much to do as they have with a Collection of medical reports or law cases'. Few critical comments could so simply identify what Wordsworth considered the essence of true poetry, where 'matters of fact' are worked upon by the transforming power of the imagination to reveal, beyond physical perception, the strange, visionary reality. More in sympathy with Wordsworth was Robert Burns (1759–96), a poet he always deeply loved. The similarity of poetic intention can be seen in the famous short poem where the ploughman-poet accidently destroys a nest of terrified field mice. The initially playful tone darkens as the tiny disaster takes on a significance for all living things. As Wordsworth wrote of Burns's poetry after his death: 'though there was no moral purpose, there is a moral effect'.

What Wordsworth settled down to do in *The Prelude*, and what no one had done before, was to try to discover exactly what happened when, between the poet on the one side and the natural world on the other, a strange fusion seemed to take place. This filled the poet with what he variously called the 'sentiment of being' (II.423), 'universal power' (II.324), 'an obscure sense / Of possible sublimity' (II.318), and so on, always searching for the perfect phrase for what at times he feared was finally inexpressible. Where did this visionary experience come from: was it something independent of man, something 'out there' in the perceived universe; was it a projection of terrors and joys from within himself upon a passive landscape; or was it a combination of the two? Whatever the answer, three things were clear: the experiences were real, they had moulded Wordsworth as the potter moulds the clay, and it was vital to record and understand them because, as the years went by, they came less and less frequently.

This dialectic between man and nature was of a kind unknown to the pastoral and landscape poetry which had preceded Wordsworth, and it was ideally suited to the spirit of the times. A. C. Bradley remarked that in 'the long poem of Wordsworth's age . . . the centre of interest is inward. It is an interest in emotion, thought, will, rather than scenes, events, actions' (*Oxford Lectures on Poetry*, 1926).

4.4 WORDSWORTH AND RELIGION

One reason why Wordsworth was able to see the relationship between man and nature as the most important and fertile subject for his poetry, was his freedom from rigid preconceptions about religion. This was particularly so in the years between 1798 and 1805 when he was writing *The Prelude*. Amid the considerable problems Wordsworth experienced during the ten years after coming down from Cambridge – politics, where to live, love, money – he was not, it seems, ever bedevilled by religious doubts. There is a remarkable contrast here with the climate of ideas which prevailed when *The Prelude* was published in mid-century. Then his successor as Poet Laureate, Alfred Tennyson, and his anthologist, Matthew Arnold, both wrote their finest poetry under the agonised pressure of religious uncertainty. 1805 was much freer from religious bigotry than 1850, but even then Wordsworth's independence of mind was very different from that of William Blake, for instance, who saw the world as caught up in perpetual warfare between the divine and the natural and believed that natural objects 'obliterate imagination' and that a religion of nature was idolatrous. Though Blake considered that Wordsworth was 'the greatest poet of his age', he also called him an 'Atheist . . . a Pagan', and told a mutual friend, Crabb Robinson, that he found Wordsworth's sublime confidence in his own mind so shocking that he had a stomach seizure which (he said) nearly killed him. As early as 1805 Coleridge had also become increasingly worried that his friend's poetry could be accused of pantheism, the doctrine that God is present in everything, so that God and Nature are identical.

Wordsworth, for the time at least, remained untroubled. His upbringing had left him with happy associations between his mother and the church at Cockermouth, with the tolerant Anglicanism of his clergymen schoolmasters at Hawkshead and with loving memories of Ann Tyson's simple meeting-house piety. And, of course, there was the constant guardian presence of his hills. It is clear that he was quite sure that he did not want to become a parson, but even at the height of his revolutionary fervour, he looked with kindly eyes on the doomed French monasteries. When he had his own family to bring up, an 1811 letter from Dorothy notes that they had, without much debate it seems, returned to church-going 'for the sake of the children'. This acceptance of traditional Anglican comfort may well have been influenced by the grief of his brother John's death. Wordsworth always disliked the narrow strictness of Evangelicals and Methodists and felt that Roman Catholicism was dominated by an intolerant priesthood. He was equally constant in his refusal to become embroiled in any of the great doctrinal debates that characterised the England of his later years. His benign point of view comes over clearly in an 1825 letter to Sir George Beaumont: 'Theologians may puzzle their heads about dogmas as they will; the Religion of gratitude cannot mislead us . . . I look abroad upon Nature, I think of the best part of our species, I lean upon my friends.'

In her essay on *The Prelude*, Helen Darbishire sums up Wordsworth's distinctive attitude towards religion: 'For him natural piety was not inconsistent with Christian piety. The two creeds stood by him side by side and when one failed the other helped.' So when Wordsworth approached his great subject – to discover where his certainty of 'a sense of sublime' came from – he was fortunately free from any inbuilt theological censorship. Instead he relied, with all the force of what Hazlitt called his 'intense intellectual egotism', upon his own mind. His faith in this was unbounded: 'Nothing can breed such fear and awe', he said, as 'the Mind of Man / My haunt and the main region of my song' (poem prefaced to *The Recluse*). In *The Prelude* Wordsworth repeatedly hails the Nature that 'has fed / My lofty speculations' (II.447–8). Such soaring confidence in the individual was in tune with Wordsworth's youth and with the revolutionary times.

We know, however, that the 'glad, confident morning' was not to survive unclouded, and as the years went by there were some significant alterations to the text of *The Prelude*. For instance, he did reorientate some, though not all, of his poem's early identifications of God with Nature. One such example occurs in Book II, lines 412–14: the early version gives the cause of his delight as 'in all things / I saw one life and felt that it was joy'; after 1839 this had been changed to 'great the joy I felt / Communing in this sort through earth and heaven / With every form of creature, as it looked / Towards the Uncreated . . .' The careful differentiation here between what is created and the 'Uncreated', i.e. God the Creator, has been seen as reflecting a more conventional attitude. But as the letter to Beaumont already shows, niceties of religious dogma were not Wordsworth's preoccupation. Though he denied that he had ever said that God and Nature were the same, what really matters to him and what manifests itself throughout *The Prelude* is the belief in an indwelling spirit which permeates the universe.

5 STYLE AND TECHNIQUE

5.1 METHOD OF COMPOSITION

Wordworth was famous among his neighbours for the way he composed his poems aloud as he walked along: 'Turble fond o' study on t'rwoads, specially at night time, and wi' a girt voice bumming away fit to flayte aw the childer to death ameast, not but what Miss Dorothy did the best part of pitting his potry togidder'. The sight of 'old Wudsworth' booming away, 'his jaws working the whoal time', was clearly a memorable one, and Wordsworth himself gives a vivid account of the embarrassments connected with his method in Book IV. 'When at evening on the public way / I sauntered like a river murmuring / And talking to itself when all things else / Are still', the household terrier who accompanied him – 'we were the happiest pair on earth' – would turn back at the sight of other walkers approaching to give his master warning. Then Wordsworth 'hushed / My voice, composed my gait' and exchanged greetings with whoever was coming, hoping thus (unsuccessfully it appears) to escape 'rumours, such as wait / On men suspected to be crazed in brain'. When he reached home, he would dictate what he had composed to his devoted womenfolk, emend, often over a long period, and at last let Dorothy or Mary make a fair copy.

This way of composing, unhindered by the labour of writing, exactly suited Wordsworth's conception of what blank verse should be like. He thought its harmony depended upon 'the apt arrangement of pauses and cadences, and the sweep of whole paragraphs', and he obviously has Milton's example in mind. There are drawbacks, however, associated with such oral composition. Speech easily conveys a great variety of emphases, pausal lengths, interpolations and climaxes which punctuation has a difficult task to imitate in print. Besides, the speaker may be tempted to prolong a sentence, readily understood by a hearer, beyond the comprehension limit of a reader; he may lose his way among a complexity of clauses, have to retrace his path, and so diminish the total effect of the period. This may have been why Tennyson complained that Wordsworth was 'too diffuse'. On the other hand, the impression of organic growth, like innumerable streams leading to one great river, which is to be found in many of Wordsworth's sentences demonstrates the irresistible power of his method of writing when it succeeds. The extraordinary three-sentence, thirty-two line paragraph of Book II, lines 419–51 illustrates this (see Section 2.3).

Like all poets of his time, Wordsworth believed in the organic nature of genius, an idea that had been gaining acceptance throughout the eighteenth century. Biological processes were seen as analogous to the development of works of art, and true genius was 'the union of unconscious and self-conscious activity, of instinct and purpose'. Keats said that 'if poetry comes not as naturally as leaves to a tree, it had better not come at all'. Blake claimed he only wrote 'when commanded by the spirits', and even that sensible lawyer Sir Walter Scott said: 'I sometimes think my fingers set up for themselves, independent of my head.' Wordsworth, in the Preface to the *Lyrical Ballads*, spoke of poetry as the 'spontaneous overflow of powerful feelings' and his chosen technique of composition ideally suited this welling inspiration. However, the strength of the original idea did not ever mean to him or to any Romantic that they need not revise what they had written. Coleridge pointed out that Shakespeare's 'judgement was at least equal' to his genius, and explained 'judgement' as 'self-consciously directing an implicit wisdom, deeper than consciousness'. Yet it may be very hard for the poet to recognise the moment when he should stop revising. A letter from Mary Wordsworth to a publisher who was being slow in producing the 1827 edition of her husband's poems, begged him to get it into print since Wordsworth was being driven 'to exhaust himself by attempting needless corrections'.

Since the time for the revision of *The Prelude* was unprecedentedly long, there has been much debate about whether revisions are necessarily improvements, and even if they are, whether they do not change the natural 'organic' form of the original inspiration. The lines immediately after the bird's-nesting episode in Book I are relevant here. In 1799 the next lines are: 'The mind of man is fashioned and built up / Even as a strain of music'. In 1805 this becomes: 'The mind of man is framed even like the breath / And harmony of music'. A final change is made in 1832, when it becomes: 'Dust as we are, the immortal spirit grows / Like harmony in music'. Most readers would agree that 1805 improves in 1799, since 'fashioned and built up' are simplified to 'framed', and 'breath and harmony' are more evocative than the conventional 'strain', but the lines are transformed and illuminated by the inversion of the initial stress in the final version. But, some readers would argue, the meaning has been changed in 1832: this sudden, traditionally Puritan reminder of the worthlessness of man – 'Dust as we are' – is quite out of keeping with the grand Wordsworthian confidence of the earlier versions in the mind of man.

5.2 CHARACTERISTIC STRUCTURES AND TECHNIQUES

Like Milton, Wordsworth organised his poem into verse paragraphs, each orchestrated round a central episode or idea. These may be linked by contrast, as when the 'all summer long' of I.424 is answered in the first line of the following paragraph by 'And in the frosty season'. Paragraph changes can mark the movement from narration and description to reflection, as when Wordsworth leaves his recollection of watching the moon rise over the sea in order to analyse just what his feelings were about nature in childhood (I.604–15). Even more emphatically, a new verse paragraph interrupts the 'listlessness' of I.266 to recall the significance of his earliest memories. Sometimes a paragraph is used to alter tempo: the speed of time and change is reflected in the brief eight-line passage (II.47–54) – 'the year span round / With giddy motion' – and this paragraph also reminds the reader of the underlying chronological impulse of the poem. The tension between this and the unpredictable, mysterious workings of memory and association is reflected in the shifting, unexpected juxtaposition of paragraphs.

The basic structure within each paragraph is blank verse, i.e. unrhymed lines of ten syllables, divided into five feet where a light is followed by a stressed syllable, a pattern clearly shown in the line:

Wĭth whíp ănd spúr wĕ thróugh thĕ cháuntr̆y fléw (II.116).

Of all verse forms, blank verse most nearly mirrors natural English speech rhythms: this basic pattern encourages endless variations to establish the poet's exact meaning and emotional emphasis. Of the various ways of doing this, Wordsworth is a master. For instance, he will use inverted stress, which not only gives variety to his verse but emphasises the shape of his argument. The paragraph starting 'If this be error, and another faith / Find easier access to the pious mind' (II.419–20) has seven clauses, each starting with 'if'. Gradually we realise that the irresistible momentum is partly due to the fact that each 'if' is marked, as by an upraised finger, with an inverted stress: 'Íf in my youth I have been pure in heart. / Íf, mingling with the world I am content'; this is repeated even when the word comes well within the line: 'The gift is yours; íf in these times of fear . . .' The organisation of stresses highlights the clausal construction, so that the clauses build up to a logical and emotional climax like a mountaineer at last achieving a longed-for peak (see Section 2.3 on this passage).

Repetition is often used, as here, to effect an interior unity within the paragraph. 'The gift is yours' is repeated later in this immensely long sentence, to be immediately followed by an echoic ' 'tis yours: the gift is yours, / Ye winds and sounding cataracts! 'tis yours, / Ye mountains! thine, O Nature!' The repetition of pronouns in the passage builds up to an equally significant pattern, with twelve first person pronouns – 'I, my, we, our' – meeting a six-fold antiphon of 'yours, ye, thine'. The total effect is not only a paean of gratitude but the suggestion of a world where Wordsworth and the mountains, winds and cataracts are all equally alive and in vivid dialogue. This illusion of dialogue characterises Wordsworth's verse. He uses direct invocation of 'the presences of Nature', the River Derwent, the 'lowly cottages' in the 'one dear vale'; he speaks to his old boyhood companions: 'Yet, my Friends! I know / That more than one of you will think of me . . .' (II.41–2) and repeatedly addresses Coleridge. Often the implicit invitation is to all his unknown readers, as he tells them to 'wonder not', or excuses the way he is fondly dwelling on his childhood memories. The cumulative effect is that of conversation rather than soliloquy, and of speaking rather than writing. Like Milton, Wordsworth often strengthens a line by the use of place names, but where Milton draws on the evocative associations of Biblical and classical sources, Wordsworth's usually come from his own country, and exceptions carry a special effect, as when the 'wolves / Howling in troops along the Bothnic Main' gives an added strangeness to the splitting ice of Esthwaite which he has named a few lines before. Direct classical references are rare and usually mock-heroic, as Vulcan (I.531) and Sabine (II.78).

Alliteration, assonance and the use of sound to echo sense, as in the wolves passage just quoted, are easily recognised and common to many poets, but two other characteristics mark Wordsworth's writing, the use of negatives and his virtuoso employment of the caesura.

Wordsworth's use of negative forms derives both from Milton and from his classical education, for negatives are a favourite Latin form, as Ovid's poems show. Negatives lend themselves to effective climaxes, when repeated 'nots' finally resolve themselves into the expected affirmative: as a result they are very popular with sermon writers. Perhaps we should remember that all ten of the school-masters at Hawkshead school when Wordsworth was there were clergymen. Negatives have another quality besides preparing for a climax, and that is opening all kinds of possibilities (see Section 6.3 for the comment on 'not unnoticed'). When Wordsworth says he deemed 'not profitless those fleeting moods' (II.312), the effect is different from saying that he found them profitable. Later in the same paragraph, where he records 'the soul, / Remembering how she felt, but what she felt / Remembering not', he does not mean that he had forgotten: he is preparing us for just how obscure is the 'obscure sense / Of possible sublimity' that he retains. In the paragraph already mentioned (II.419–52) there is a great variety of negative forms. Apart from 'despair not' and 'fail not', which carry different overtones from 'be cheerful' or 'succeed', there is the implied negative of 'were I destitute', and phrases of open possibilities like 'disguised in gentle names', and it is interesting to notice how 'never-failing' in the last line but one achieves an effect of promise that could not be equalled by any positive term.

Wordsworth's attempt to read 'deeply in the history of his own mind' was a difficult one, and we know the infinite care he always gave to his choice of words. A visitor in 1830 was struck by his 'spirit of rectitude . . . he spoke as though he was always upon oath' like 'some members of the Society of Friends I had known'. An 1829 letter describes words as 'not a mere vehicle but . . . powers either to kill or animate'. Wordsworth's negative forms, then, carry a special assurance of sincerity: he uses them because he then can tell us what things are not, even if it is impossible, within the limits of language, to say exactly what they are. The conclusion of the borrowed boat episode (I.390–400) provides a powerful example of this.

The iambic line is often marked by a strong central pause called a caesura: 'I cannot miss my way. / I breathe again' (I.18) is an uncomplicated example. Of course, if the caesura were always placed centrally, the verse would sound dead; Wordsworth loves a variously divided line and the division may fall anywhere or be withheld. He uses it to divide his clauses, to underline a repetition, or to impart to an abstract idea the vitality of conversation, revealing a rhythmic control that is one of the great joys of his verse, as in:

> already I began
> To love the sun; / a boy I loved the sun,
> Not as I since have loved him, / as a pledge
> And surety of our earthly life, / a light
> Which we behold / and feel we are alive;
> Nor for his bounty to so many worlds –
> But for this cause, / that I had seen him lay
> His beauty on the morning hills, / had seen . . . (II.177–83)

5.3 IMAGERY

In the prologue to *The Excursion*, Wordsworth exclaimed 'How exquisitely the human mind . . . to the external world is fitted'. Belief in such unity between his mind and the external world is central to Wordsworth's imagery, for he was quite sure that imagery could only be justified at all if it sprang 'from the strong creative power of human passion' (see Section 3.3). It must have the same organic inevitability that appears in the developing awareness of the new-born child and which he actually calls the 'first Poetic spirit' (II.260–1).

A densely figurative passage occurs in Book II, lines 200–15 which we can use as a (fairly!) straightforward example of Wordsworth's combination of simile, metaphor and personification:

> . . . I hasten on to tell
> How nature, intervenient till this time
> And secondary, now at length was sought
> For her own sake. But who shall parcel out
> His intellect by geometric rules,
> Split like a province into round and square?
> Who knows the individual hour in which
> His habits were first sown, even as a seed?
> Who that shall point as with a wand and say
> This portion of the river of my mind
> Came from yon fountain? Thou, my Friend! art one
> More deeply read in thy own thoughts; to thee
> Science appears but what in truth she is,
> Not as our glory and our absolute boast,
> But as a succedaneum and a prop
> To our infirmity.

In personification, an idea or an inanimate object is given an illusion of life, often by imputing to it human thoughts or feelings. Here both Nature (201) and Science (212) are to be personified; the first appears as a friend who has always been visited occasionally but who now has become fascinating in herself. Science (here probably meaning all consciously acquired learning) is treated differently, since the impression of personality implied in 'she' appears only for a moment. Why is this? It is because Wordsworth has come to agree with Coleridge that Science is not a living force, like Nature, but only a means by which that living force may be studied. So Wordsworth now uses an intentionally pedantic simile 'as a succedaneum and a prop'. A simile depends on an explicit comparison between two things, here 'Science' and 'succedaneum/prop', which clearly carries a demotion in importance, making it sound extraordinarily dull.

Meanwhile line 203 asks the first of three rhetorical questions, rhetorical here because Wordsworth knows that no one can possibly answer them. All three enquire how we can be precise about what has made us the way we are, and each uses a different metaphor. The term 'metaphor' implies rather than states a comparison, and it is useful to employ the word 'tenor' for the subject and 'vehicle' for the metaphor itself. So in the first question the tenor is the analysis of the intellect and the vehicle is geometry; in the second the tenor is individual habit and the vehicle is gardening; the third implies two tenors, the variation and the origin of the mind, and uses two associated vehicles, river and fountain.

The passage has further complications in that the first question adds the simile 'like a province', so that a geographical map image is imposed on the geometric figure, the second adds a psalm-like echo to 'sown' with the simile 'as a seed', and the third has an enquiring 'Who', which is virtually a personification of a lecturer complete with 'wand' or pointer to demonstrate something on a blackboard. Of course, there are many words which hover between metaphor and accepted idiom, such as 'split' and 'parcel out'. The more one studies this passage, the more it can be seen as fulfilling its task of sharing with the reader Wordsworth's actual situation. Here he is demonstrating the impossibility of intellectualising the history of his mind: the complexity of his figurative language evolves from the labyrinth of uncertainty as he treads 'the shadowy ground of his own past'. He has not produced these figures of speech as ornaments, but they have emerged organically out of his subject.

More elusive is the way in which Wordsworth's description of landscape or narration of events itself modulates into an image, or when the juxtaposition of image and reality is so intricate that the poem hangs like a dream or a mirage between imagination and fact, as in the journey at the opening of *The Prelude*. Coleridge saw Wordsworth's images as 'like a green field reflected in a calm and perfectly transparent lake'. This is an inspired description of the unobtrusive movement in the poem between literal and figurative, and exactly suits many of the episodes in the poem where the landscape and the situation are conveyed with great particularity, but quite suddenly the reader realises the focus has shifted so that the 'real' landscape has assumed a metaphorical significance.

The borrowed boat episode is of this pattern, the dreams which afterwards haunt the boy acting as a metaphysical reflection of the original landscape. The same pattern recurs in the flute-player/island passage (II.164–74). The island is real and the boy really did play the flute, but by line 170 the landscape has become visionary, 'like a dream'. In Wordsworth's night walks (II.302–23), the actuality is the poet sheltering from the endless Lakeland rain under a projecting rock and hearing the strange sounds made by the wind and the soaking earth, but these noises turn into a communication beyond ordinary language. In the skating scene the vitality of the skater becomes transferred to the universe around him; on his early morning walk the effect of the utter solitude of the vale is that 'bodily eyes / Were utterly forgotten, and what I saw / Appeared like something in myself, a dream, / A prospect in the mind'. Again and again he speaks of his own 'creative sensibility', his 'plastic power', and of an 'auxiliar light' which 'came from my mind'. 'The midnight storm', he says, 'grew darker in the presence of my eye'. This power was with him from his earliest years: he was only ten when 'I felt / Gleams like the flashing of a shield; – the earth / And common face of Nature spake to me / Rememberable things'.

Certain elements in Wordsworth's landscapes recur so frequently that one is reminded of Blake's need to create his own myth system to give him a framework for his longer poems, or of Coleridge's similar impulse in 'The Ancient Mariner'. Wordsworth's landscape is transmuted from the actual counties of Cumberland and Westmorland into a myth country where giant mountains pursue travellers, where wind and earth speak an ancient language, or where 'some floating thing / Upon the river' (I.29–30) may be the guide for the hero's quest.

Two dominant and animating images are those of wind and water. The poem begins with Wordsworth's renewed experience of the life-giving wind, which can change to a tempest (I.37), become an Aeolian harp (I.96), hold the boy 'suspended' when bird's-nesting, and lift or dash his kite as unpredictably as the breath of inspiration comes or goes. Water runs endlessly through the poem, in cataracts, streams, lakes, rivers and the sea. Indeed, there is a very striking passage at the beginning of Book IX which speaks of the whole poem as a river, constantly turning back upon itself because of its fear of being 'engulphed . . . in the ravenous sea'. The first certainty about the subject of Wordsworth's poem comes to him with the voice of the River Derwent, whose sound 'flowed along' his childhood dreams, and these water images are often transformed by light. One of his earliest memories (I.564–6) is of waters interfused with light – 'silver wreaths / Of curling mist' – and he is fascinated by the way the sea changes with the rising of the moon (I.566–80). Light can be an image of beauty, of the love linking man with Nature and of the activity of the creative mind. 'I loved the sun . . . the moon to me was dear', he chases the reflection of a star as he skates, and at other times he feels that his mind 'on the image of the setting sun / Bestowed new splendour' (II.369–70).

Mountains are such continuously powerful images that some commentators have suggested that they acted as surrogate parents for the orphaned Wordsworth. It is his joy 'To range the open heights', he watches the distant hills for the first sign of the rising moon (I.571), hears them send 'an alien sound / Of melancholy back' to the skaters, and there is the famous avenging 'huge peak, black and huge' which rears its head when he is in the borrowed boat. The climax of the poem will be the ascent by night of a mountain, Snowdon, where the search for understanding which started with Book I will at last be satisfied.

The pattern of Wordsworth's presentation of his memories, with landscape transforming into another, visionary world, which may in turn be succeeded by an understanding 'Beyond the reach of thought / And human Knowledge, to the human eye / Invisible' (II.403–5) is linked with the central purpose of the poem. This is to prove, by his own evidence, that man has a 'filial bond' with Nature, that this unity can be glimpsed through the beauty and terror of the external world, and that it will provide 'A never-failing principle of joy'. In technical terms, the tenor is the strange, joyous unity between man and Nature, the vehicle is the experienced landscape of Wordsworth's youth.

6 CRITICAL ANALYSIS

6.1 ANALYSING PASSAGES FROM *THE PRELUDE*

Few poets complain so much as Wordsworth about the difficulty of making language do what he wanted. Near the beginning of *The Prelude* he contrasts 'the mind's internal echo' with the 'imperfect sound' of the actual language. He is not alone in this complaint. In *Poetry in the Making*, Ted Hughes speaks about words as 'tools with which we try to give some part of our experience a more or less permanent shape outside ourselves' but 'far from ideal for their job'. Philip Larkin, in *The Pleasure Principle*, calls writing poetry a 'highly contradictory activity . . . the conscious organization of an unconscious impulse', and names three stages in writing a poem: the initial obsessive idea the 'emotional concept', the tremendously hard work of getting this idea into words, and then the individual reading of the poem. This last again connects with Wordsworth and his definition of a poet: 'a man speaking to men'.

So the task that every reader inherits from the poet is that of trying to understand just what he is doing with his words: what effects he thinks he is achieving by his metrical scheme and by his variations upon it, why he ends his lines with one word and not another, why he describes this scene and not that, what he is making his imagery and his diction do, where he employs repetition and where contrast, what 'special effects' like alliteration or inversion he may use and why. The more the poet's language is explored, the nearer the reader approaches what Hughes calls the 'mansions inside the head', Larkin the 'emotional concept', and Wordsworth 'the mind's internal echo'. Only when the meaning is understood can the writer's technique be appreciated, but only by studying technique can we comprehend what the writer is trying to do. And as you will soon find, however much you discover, a later reading will always reveal more.

In studying a verse-paragraph from *The Prelude*, we first need to recognise how it fits into the whole: whether it is a narration or description that has its genesis in some special experience and will then develop from this; or whether it is a linking paragraph in which Wordsworth reflects upon the cumulative effect of many experiences, or considers how memory operates, or traces the way a new-born baby establishes an unconscious sympathy with the world around her.

In each case, one needs to focus the movement within the passage: it may move from companionship to solitude, from one point in time to another, perhaps years distant, or there may be a great change in mood (as in the flute-player episode), often from noise to silence, or a change in weather or season.

Often the opening of the paragraph will be precise, as in the bird's-nesting description, but it will move towards suggestion, and often, too, the reader will then notice a marked withdrawal of the strong physical, sensuous impressions that have initiated the passage. Far from ending with a celebration of the beauty of nature, there will be the feeling of strangeness, of another dimension, as at the end of the borrowed boat episode. We realise that somewhere during the passage the description of what is happening in the world we see around us has become instead an image of forces operating upon the human mind and – equally important – from within the mind.

It seems to be the special function of the narrative passages to fuse nature and mind in this way, and it is useful to watch how this is engineered by the way clauses are organised within sentences and sentences within the paragraph (see Section 4.3 and the commentary on II.419–51). Remember that the techniques used – repetition, contrast, inversion, negative forms, invocation, change from matter of fact diction to abstract – are by conscious intention of the poet in his struggle to put over his 'unconscious impulse'.

There may be different levels of time within a paragraph, as the older Wordsworth looks back on his young self and tries to understand how memory works. He remarks on the difficulty of this at the beginning of Book II: 'so wide appears / The vacancy between me and those days / . . . often do I seem / Two consciousnesses'; how this will affect the actual language used shows in the description of the moon rising over the sea. Wordsworth points out that his younger self would have been 'a stranger' to the images he now employs.

Wordsworth gives energy to many passages by his facility in choosing verbs of action. There is a dramatically effective use of present participle forms in I.539–43 – 'splitting . . . struggling . . . yelling . . . howling' – to mark the contrast between the domestic comfort of the cottage interior and the fierce forces of nature all around. Less obvious is the way the infant baby passage is animated by the action of 'nurse . . . sinks . . . rocked . . . drinks', all within two and a half lines. Sometimes a special effect arises from juxtaposing words from different sources of the English language: 'Scudding away from snare to snare' is dominated by Saxon words, but the continuation 'I plied / That anxious visitation' has three words of Latin origin. The first part vividly suggests a boy's energetic activity, the second superimposes an adult reflection.

Diction joins with metre, alliteration and assonance to evoke sensuous experience: in 'the shuddering ivy dripped large drops' (II.124), notice how the three heavy consecutive stresses join with the alliterative 'd's and 'p's to suggest what it describes. Similarly, 'We beat with thundering hoofs the level sand' uses insistently regular iambic metre and exact diction to produce an image that is aural and tactile as well as visual.

The same passage also illustrates the need for close reading to get the full effect of contrast in II.108–12. The form is a,b,a – peace, tumult, peace – but look how carefully the reader must follow the construction both of syntax and of vision. The eye must travel up from the peace of the valley to the wild west wind sweeping overhead from the Irish Sea and then back to the contrast of the silent motionless trees, motionless as the towers in the deep valley. Otherwise the suggestion of 'more than inland' is lost: this is not just out of the wind but something special, magical like the stone circles, or the ruined abbey just mentioned. The same shape of contrast can be seen in the description of the Windermere tavern: lines 142–4 describe 'a splendid place, the door beset / With chaises, grooms and liveries, and within / Decanters, glasses and the blood-red wine', and later there is a description of the gaudy 'spangled' new inn-sign. Neatly between, Wordsworth inserts a single line describing the simple hut that this brash new place has supplanted: 'Proud of its one bright fire and sycamore shade.'

Wordsworth said in a letter of 1831: 'the composition of verse is infinitely more of an art than men are prepared to believe, and absolute success in it depends upon innumerable minutiae'. One such detail is the way Wordsworth orientates a line round a repetition: 'Frail creature as he is, helpless as frail' shows how the emphatic positioning and heavy stress of the repeated 'frail' is intensified by the synonym 'helpless', the whole effect being analogous to the effect of a single sustained note in a piece of music. Even the word 'and' is used with special care; John Jones says Wordsworth uses it more frequently than any other poet, preserving 'structural simplicity' and conveying 'an insistence on the particular', as in 'O'er all that leaps and runs and shouts and sings' (II.406).

Many commentators have noticed the subtle effects gained by Wordsworth's manipulation of line-ending. For instance, Christopher Ricks calls attention to the conclusion of the borrowed boat episode: 'No familiar shapes / Remained, no pleasant images of trees, / Of sea or sky, no colours of green fields; / But huge and mighty forms, that do not live / Like living men . . .' Here the tiny pause before the eye travels on to the next line suggests to the reader that these 'huge and mighty forms' have some sort of mysterious existence that yet is 'not living'. Then the completion of the clause with 'like living men' builds upon a feeling of strangeness and dread already established in the mind. Similarly, at the end of II.407 the word 'glides' seems to belong to the wing of a bird suggested earlier in the line by 'beat the gladsome air' – but no, the reader finds the next line 'Beneath the wave': the impression is that of a seabird diving.

The student of *The Prelude* may be confident about one thing: the more closely he reads, the greater will be his pleasure.

6.2 SPECIMEN PASSAGE (I.425–63)

And in the frosty season, when the sun   425
Was set, and visible for many a mile
The cottage windows blazed through twilight gloom,
I heeded not their summons: happy time
It was indeed for all of us – for me
It was a time of rapture! Clear and loud   430
The village clock tolled six, – I wheeled about,
Proud and exulting like an untired horse
That cares not for his home. All shod with steel,
We hissed along the polished ice in games
Confederate, imitative of the chase   435
And woodland pleasures, – the resounding horn,
The pack loud chiming, and the hunted hare.
So through the darkness and the cold we flew,
And not a voice was idle; with the din
Smitten, the precipices rang aloud;   440
The leafless trees and every icy crag
Tinkled like iron; while far distant hills
Into the tumult sent an alien sound
Of melancholy not unnoticed, while the stars
Eastward were sparkling clear, and in the west   445
The orange sky of evening died away.
Not seldom from the uproar I retired
Into a silent bay, or sportively
Glanced sideway, leaving the tumultuous throng,
To cut across the reflex of a star   450
That fled, and, flying still before me, gleamed
Upon the glassy plain; and oftentimes,
When we had given our bodies to the wind,
And all the shadowy banks on either side
Came sweeping through the darkness, spinning still   455
The rapid line of motion, then at once
Have I, reclining back upon my heels,

Stopped short; yet still the solitary cliffs
Wheeled by me – even as if the earth had rolled
With visible motion her diurnal round!   460
Behind me did they stretch in solemn train,
Feebler and feebler, and I stood and watched
Till all was tranquil as a dreamless sleep.

6.3 CRITICAL ANALYSIS

The passage begins with a sharply focused winter landscape, seen at a specific moment. There is intense awareness of physical activity: sight, sound, touch, motion and companionship are powerfully evoked. It ends in silence, solitude and stillness, with the visible world fading into a 'dreamless sleep'. This is one of a series of descriptions of the 'exercise and play' of the young Wordsworth which record an enviable range of boyhood delights in all weathers and seasons, both alone and with a crowd of friends. Looking back, the adult Wordsworth recognises these episodes as educating him 'alike by beauty and by fear'. In each case the movement is from precise statement towards implication and surmise of such importance that ever afterwards he retains 'an obscure sense of possible sublimity' (II.317–18).

What, then, was so important about this frosty evening on Esthwaite or Windermere? Typically, the paragraph starts with Wordsworth's 'And', unifying the experience he is about to recount with the summer fields just before; and with three light syllables which impart an indefinable air of speed and joy to the line, that quality in Wordsworth's verse which one critic has described as like skating light and swift over thin ice. Time is exactly established, first by the light: the sun has set, but it is not yet night, so it is possible to identify the cottages whose windows 'blaze' through the gloom. 'Blaze' suggests a force of warmth as well as of light, pleasure in human contact, but Wordsworth no sooner establishes this than in line 428 he rejects it: the 'heeded not' is picked up by the alliteration of 'happy', and the union of the two ideas is accepted in the shared heedless happiness of all the 'noisy crew'. Yet the opening sentence will end on a carefully organised differentiation between Wordsworth and his schoolmates, centring round the contrasted 'for all of us – for me': 'happy' for them but 'rapture' for him, the latter word receiving all the emphasis of caesura and end of sentence. Note, too, Wordsworth's repetition here to establish contrast, particularly since it relies on his favourite verb 'to be'.

Time has been established by the light; now it is established by sound, as we hear the village clock in the emphatic monosyllables of

430–1. 'I wheeled about' echoes the pattern of 'I heeded not', with the effect that not a moment has elapsed between the two, but that rapture, tolling bell, wheeling about are instantaneous, and this is intensified in the insistent physicality of the horse simile. The horse is 'untired', i.e. Wordsworth is using a negative form, with its special capacity for suggestion, since there is a half-realised pointer that others at this time of day perhaps might be tired, but not *this* horse/boy. Again the independence of 'heeded not' is echoed in 'cares not for his home'. The impression of activity increases in a crescendo of action and sound. Like horses, they are all shod with metal, and 'steel' lends its sibilant to the fourfold sibilation of the next line, producing an illusion of speed. The group of schoolboys has become a pack of hunters with hounds and hare: somebody mimics the 'resounding horn', while 'chiming' here is the term for the varied voices of baying hounds. It is dark by now on the level of the lake (438) and the speed intensifies further with the suggestion of birds 'flew', but equally vivid is the din, and this now passes from human/brass/animal sound to evoke the response of the whole frozen world: precipices, trees, crag, far distant hills all join in the extraordinary dialogue. As with the voices from the lake, the voices from the surrounding landscape are all different – rang, tinkled like iron, a melancholy sound – and their evocation uses the echoic quality of assonance: 'dim/smitten', 'leafless trees', 'every icy', as well as the more obvious onomatopoeia.

It is at this moment of the fusion of the human and the natural world that a change comes over the tone and tempo of the passage. It is only on rereading that we realise that the change is initiated half-way through both paragraph and sentence, with two clauses both introduced by 'while'. As the *Oxford Dictionary* points out, the force of 'while' depends on something else happening at the same time, and very often something else in marked contrast.

The first marked contrast here is the different sound sent back by the 'far distant hills'. In what way is it different? It is alien, it is a sound of melancholy, and it is 'not unnoticed'. All three qualities provide their own complexity, for instance we do not know whether Wordsworth is the only one who has this reaction. More important is the typical combination of precision and vagueness. Alien not only suggests difference, strangeness, but carries an inimical overtone (notice the way the word has been picked up by science fiction). The melancholy is unexplained: we simply do not know why some sounds, for instance minor keys, have this strange effect. 'Not unnoticed' is typical of Wordsworth's negative (here double negative) form, leaving the reader with the boundaries instead of the substance of his reaction. That is to say, if 'noticing' is in a scale of 1 to 10, with indifference at the lower end and shock at the top, Wordsworth's reaction is fairly low down. We can argue that the reader accepts this because of the previous precision: we are implicitly called upon to know, in these circumstances, how alert but diverted our attention would be.

The second 'while' contrast is quite different in effect: the over-arching span of time is caught up from the sunset of the first line to the final dying away of evening colour in the west, so that the stars now show clearly. The majestic passage of time across the sky has continued unobserved during the tumult on the lake; 'sparkling' reminds us of the frost, and the stars are going to provide the second impulse of the paragraph, as it moves from noisy, unthinking sociable delight to Wordsworth seeking silence and solitude – 'I retired / Into a silent bay'. It is at this point that the observed scene begins to take on the characteristic further implications of an image. Young Words-worth really is chasing the image of a star reflected in the ice (Wordsworth was always a very good skater) but that he does so at this moment, and continues to do so even though he knows his quest is for the unattainable, since the 'reflex' will change its position just as fast as he does, is also a metaphor for his life-long attempt to 'see into the heart of things'. The image of pursuing a star is as old as myth itself, the star being a symbol of what is wanted, what can be seen but never held. There is here, too, a typical exchange of roles between man and nature – the star now is 'fled and flying', as the skaters were a few lines before. Again it is typical that Wordsworth leaves this image after two and a half lines to superimpose another in which man and the universe interact – the reader has to get used to this rapid replacement of ideas. He complained bitterly about the 'sad incom-petence of human speech' (VI.593). One of his palliatives seems to be imitating the constant movement of nature by a mimetic movement of image.

The same see-saw between reality and image, precision and implication comes with Wordsworth's next enterprise when, having worked up tremendous speed by skating with the wind behind him, he abruptly stops. The abruptness is mirrored in placing, time construction and stress: the 'at once' lies at the end of the line: what will happen? The next line starts with an auxiliary verb and subject, but again the main verb is delayed until yet another line, with two emphatic stresses 'stopped short'. The sentence continues with two and a half smoothly propelled lines, subject followed by irresistible predicate as the cliffs appear to sweep on past his eyes so that he seems to witness the actual rotation of the earth, a feeling underlined by the echo between 'rolled' and 'round'. Now it is the cliffs which 'wheeled' as he had done at the beginning of the passage. The reader realises the 'minutiae' of Wordsworth's art by understanding the careful selection of the adjective 'solitary' for the cliffs (458): no one is on them, they are deserted, but also they are individual –this is a series of headlands, not a continuous cliff.

The final three lines act as a coda, with the initial preposition 'Behind' signalling both place and time, for the experience, physical and psychic, is past. Here again the language operates in two contrary directions at once. The cliffs are simultaneously impressive – 'in solemn train' – but now also scarcely visible, and/or the illusion of their movement is dying away, so they are 'feebler and feebler'. Once more it is the poet who is at the centre of things – 'I stood and watched' – accepting the post-visionary quietude of the hypnotic last line, where 'tranquil' is anticipated by the similar sounds of 'till all'. The final simile of 'as a dreamless sleep' ends both noise and movement.

What is the mood of this ending? The whole passage is full of juxtapositions between indoors and outdoors, company and solitude, west and east, firelight, sunlight, starlight, motion and stillness, circular and linear movement, noise and silence, noise and echo, substance and shadow, reality and illusion and, centrally, between the individual and the natural world. In the 'tumult' of the passage there seems to have been, if not a union, a kind of cosmic dance between two partners, of enormous vitality and importance. At the end the melancholy, the alien sound seems to re-establish its voice with the acceptance of silence and the implications of 'dreamless sleep'.

7 CRITICAL RESPONSES

The long-delayed publication of *The Prelude* means that there is little contemporary critical evaluation. In an 1804 letter to Sir George Beaumont, Wordsworth defines the subject of the poem as 'the growth of my own mind taken up on a large scale' and reveals his uneasiness about its length, wondering if it ought to be 'lopped'. Yet the next sentence recognises that abbreviation is impossible: cut out odd bits of his interlaced reflections and memories and *The Prelude* would no longer make sense. Neither Coleridge nor de Quincey shared his fears about length. When Wordsworth read the 1805 version to Coleridge, he immediately gave vent to his admiration in a moving 120-line poem. To him it was the absolute warranty of Wordsworth's poetic greatness: 'Of Truth profound a sweet continuous song', he says. Coleridge accurately observes the nerve centres of the poem, the effect upon the growing boy of the delights and terrors of his early environment and upon the young man of those tempestuous years when 'France in all her towns lay vibrating'. De Quincey's reaction was equally appreciative, especially of the poem's visionary nature, and his frequent enthusiastic references meant that the existence of this poem 'of high pretensions and extraordinary magnitude' became widely known.

Unfortunately, while *The Prelude* lay unpublished in Wordsworth's desk for forty-five years, critical estimation of his work had settled into a mould that made recognition of the complex originality of this poem unlikely. (A similar situation might be imagined if the publication of T. S. Eliot's 1922 poem, *The Waste Land*, had been delayed until the 1970s.) What was admired as particularly Wordsworthian was a simple, direct appreciation of nature and reverence for the affections and duties of family life. John Ruskin in 1843 is typical, too, in hailing Wordsworth as a moral leader to be 'trusted as a guide in everything, he feels nothing but what we all ought to feel . . . he says nothing but what we all ought to believe'.

When *The Prelude*, beautifully printed, did at last appear in 1850 the reaction of the reviews fell into three main categories. It is difficult to believe that some, particularly the *Edinburgh Magazine*, had read it at all, so totally do the comments ignore both the complex organisation of the poem and Wordsworth's vision of a nature informed as much by terror as by beauty. The 'texture of the composition' is described as 'in general eminently artless'; it is 'a tale of childhood, boyhood and youth, tranquil, happy and innocent'. Much more to the point are the *Gentleman's Magazine*, the *Eclectic* and the *Examiner*, who all detect an essential solitariness, a lack of 'deep and vital sympathy with men, their works and ways' in Wordsworth's 'journey into the history of his mind'. They complain that he 'is always the prominent, often the exclusive, object of his song'. The comparisons with other poets of his time are to Wordsworth's disadvantage: Byron is more exciting, Cowper has humour, Shelley shows more fury with political injustice and, above all, in both Shelley and Goethe 'we encounter in its full vigour the erotic element of poetry, the absence of which in Wordsworth is so remarkable'.

The most perceptive of the reviews, however, often combine these reactions with a recognition of the original, experimental nature of the poem: 'the first regular, versified autobiography', says the *Eclectic*, and the *Gentleman's Magazine* gives proper importance to the traumatic impact upon Wordsworth of the French Revolution: 'an electric shock to his whole spiritual being, pervasive in its immediate and permanent in its remote effects. It led him to meditate on the destinies and capabilities of man; upon the powers and duties of the poet; upon the relationships of society and nature.' The poem is admired for being 'so rich in both historical and psychological interest'. The use of the word 'psychological' is interesting. It would have been unfamiliar or unknown to Wordsworth when he was writing the poem; when Coleridge used it in 1818 he felt he ought to apologise for such an invention, saying 'it is one of which our language stands in great need'. By 1850 it had clearly become the 'in' word, and it is the psychological element that attracts most admiration. *Graham's Magazine* sees that 'topics, trite in themselves are all made original from the peculiarities of the person conceiving them . . . few metaphysicians ever scanned their consciousness with more intensity of vision . . . *The Prelude* contains more real knowledge of man's internal constitution than can be found in Hume or Kant.'

In spite of this recognition there is a pervasive feeling that the poem, though remarkable, belongs to the past: 'It seems a large fossil relic – imperfect and magnificent – newly dug up and with the fresh soil and the old dim subsoil meeting and mingling round it.' By 1850, of course, the dominant form had become the novel, with the concomitant effect that all the successful long poems such as Tennyson's *The Princess* or Elizabeth Barrett Browning's *Aurora Leigh* used a strong narrative structure, and even short poems were often cast as dramatic monologues. The psychological perception that was recognised and saluted in *The Prelude* was now being explored in these more popular forms.

The poem fared no better for the remainder of the century. In 1870 Matthew Arnold published a selection of Wordsworth which concentrated on the lyrics and shorter narratives, excluding *The Prelude* which Arnold considered was 'by no means Wordsworth's best work'. So it remained largely unread until, in 1909, the critic A. C. Bradley re-established it as central to Wordsworth's art. Bradley shows how Arnold, in his eagerness to make Wordsworth popular, represented his poetry 'as much more simple and unambitious than it really was and as much more easily apprehended than it ever can be'. Bradley picks up the quality that had so impressed de Quincey: that of sublimity, when beauty is united with terror. He sees clearly how absolute a bond exists between Wordsworth's early environment and the way he sees the world: for him, natural objects, though perceived with more than usual intensity, always appear against a background of 'unknown modes of being'. Nor is this experience tranquillising: it 'comes with a distinct shock, which may bewilder, confuse or trouble the mind, and it is specially associated with mountains and with solitude'. Of the scene in Book XII, where the boy Wordsworth waited on a bare hillside for the horses to take him home, Bradley says 'everything here is natural, but everything is apocalyptic'.

Bradley made the reader aware that it was not enough to see Wordsworth as a reassuring and high-minded celebrant of nature. Indeed, he argues that it was only Dorothy's influence, after the trauma of his French Revolution experiences, that directed him towards 'unassuming, sympathetic, domestic poetry'. To read *The Prelude*, says Bradley, is to be made aware of his disturbing sense of strangeness, his visionary power: 'He apprehended all things, natural or human, as the expression of something, which, while manifested in them, immeasurably transcends them.'

Intelligent understanding of the poem was facilitated by the 1926 publication, in parallel texts, of the 1805 and 1850 versions, followed in the 1970s by the two-book version of 1799. The rewritings, omissions and additions provide fascinating evidence of changes in Wordsworth's style and thought over fifty years. In her review of the 1926 edition, the critic Helen Darbishire pointed out how a 'more decorated, literary form' sometimes replaces the earlier version with its 'naked language' springing 'straight out of the experience itself', and how 'revolutionary politics will be checked and moral and religious conceptions' adjusted to avoid imputations of socialism or pantheism. In common with many recent critics, Darbishire prefers the earliest texts, where 'elemental experience [is] freed from the gloss of later interpretation', the roots of this experience lying 'where Wordsworth did not shrink from finding them, in the sensuous or animal life which is our common heritage'. This characteristic she explicitly connects with twentieth-century poetry.

Understanding of the poem was also increased by biographical studies, such as the 1922 work of G. M. Harper and E. Legouis, who concentrated on the year Wordsworth had spent in France, his connections with Beaupuy and the Girondists, and the ill-fated love affair with Annette. All this provided an invaluable counterbalance to Arnold's presentation of Wordsworth as a tranquil poet of reassurance. Instead the reader could now focus him engulfed in a singularly violent and tumultuous age and understand the force of despair that had driven him to write *The Prelude* at all. Another important book which meshed together life and poetry was W. M. Margoliouth's *Wordsworth and Coleridge*, which teases out the ways in which the writing of *The Prelude* was influenced by the younger poet.

There has been much stimulating discussion of Wordsworth's use of language. For instance, Christopher Ricks's 1971 essay, *A Pure Organic Pleasure from the Lines*, demonstrates the insight that can be gained from studying individual words like 'hung' in the bird's-nesting sequence, and the manipulation of line/sentence endings in the skating episode. Wordsworth's use of images has proved a very rewarding topic. Darbishire had already noticed in 1926 how the 'literal becomes figurative and then literal again'. Herbert Lindenberger's *On Wordsworth's Prelude* connects this interaction with the way his apparently straightforward, factual descriptions can reveal themselves as symbols typical of those used by many Romantic writers. Other critics, like W. B. Gallie (1947), return to the question of whether *The Prelude* is a philosophical poem (he decides it is, because it 'creates the struggle of thought').

What the wealth of recent discussion has done is to challenge the oddly persistent image offered by Arnold, and replace it by that of a visionary poet, born into a period of extreme social turmoil, unusually aware of a world whose magnificence was only equalled by its strangeness, and whose methods and techniques of exploring his dilemma are as original and difficult as they are rewarding to study.

REVISION QUESTIONS

1. Wordsworth said he had been 'fostered alike by beauty and by fear'. Using three episodes from *The Prelude*, Books I and II, show what he meant by this.

2. Wordsworth had a very strong sense of his vocation as a poet. By what means does he convey this in the first two books of *The Prelude*?

3. Images based on wind and water pervade *The Prelude*. Discuss the varied ways in which they are used.

4. What did Wordsworth mean by 'spots of time'? Using episodes from both books show why these were so important to him.

5. With close reference to the text, show how Wordsworth's descriptions of his boyhood start with precise statement but end 'in surmise'.

6. What do you think are Wordsworth's most striking qualities as a poet?

7. Briefly recount two of the episodes which Wordworth recalls from his boyhood. Then show in detail how he makes them so vivid.

8. *The Prelude* was intended as no more than 'evidence of Wordsworth's qualifications to write a masterpiece he never wrote'. Explain briefly under what circumstances he wrote *The Prelude*, why it exists in different versions, and why it was not published in his lifetime.

9. 'Even Wordsworth's most elevated moods are deeply rooted in the world of sense.' Choose two or three examples of such 'elevated moods' and discuss this judgement.

10. Between 1799 and 1805 Wordsworth altered the beginning of Book I, adding the 269 lines leading up to 'Was it for this . . . ?' What was the 'this' that needed so much explanation?

11. According to Wordsworth, *The Prelude* describes 'the growth of a poet's mind'. What do we learn about this growth from the first two books of the poem?

FURTHER READING

The student of *The Prelude* Books I and II will get considerable help from reading two early poems of Wordsworth: the 'Lines Composed a Few Miles above Tintern Abbey' (1798) and the ode on 'Intimations of Immortality from the Recollections of Early Childhood' (1798). The passages which were moved from the original 1799 version to later books of the extended poem are also well worth reading: these are Book V, lines 426–59 (the drowned man), Book XI, lines 208–61 (the gibbet), Book XI, lines 287–335 (waiting for the horses). Book IX, lines 510–30 has the conversation with Beaupuy, and Book XIV, lines 1–62 the climax of the poem with the night-time ascent of Snowdon.

The poem is so bound up with Wordsworth's life that reading about him and his circle is illuminating. The best short book is *Wordsworth and Coleridge 1795–1834* by W. M. Margoliouth (Oxford University Press, 1953). The standard life is by Mary Moorman: *Wordsworth, a Biography* (Oxford University Press, 1957 and 1965). This is quite long (two volumes) but is very readable and full of fascinating detail, providing a useful parallel to Wordsworth's account of events in the poem. Alan Hill has edited selections of letters: *Letters of Dorothy Wordsworth* and *Letters of William Wordsworth*, both in Oxford Paperbacks, 1984. The very recently discovered letters between William and his wife have cast a new light upon him unglimpsed by earlier biographers: *The Love Letters of William and Mary Wordsworth*, edited by Beth Darlington (Chatto and Windus, 1982). Wordsworth's own *Guide to the Lakes* has been republished by Oxford Paperbacks, 1977, and *The Lake District: an Anthology*, compiled by Norman Nicholson (Penguin Books, 1982), includes a lot about Wordsworth and brings his countryside vividly to life.

The best text for the student is the *Norton Critical Edition: The Prelude: 1799, 1805, 1850*, edited by Jonathan Wordsworth, M. H. Abrams and Stephen Gill, 1979. This gives the little-known 1799 version and then the 1805 and 1850 versions in parallel texts and with generous footnotes; it also has a useful selection of recent critical essays. The *Penguin Critical Anthology, William Wordsworth*, edited by Graham McMaster, 1972, contains a wide selection of the first reviews of *The Prelude*, selections from the important essays by Bradley and Darbishire, and more recent work on Wordsworth. A range of modern approaches is to be found in the Macmillan Casebook Series on *The Prelude*, edited by W. J. Harvey and R. Gravil, and in M. H. Abrams's *Wordsworth: A Collection of Critical Essays* (Prentice-Hall, 1972). The same author's *The Mirror and the Lamp* (Norton, 1958) provides an invaluable background to the ideas of the Romantic Movement, as does Basil Willey's *Eighteenth Century Background* (Chatto and Windus, 1940) to Wordsworth's ideas about nature.

Mastering English Literature
Richard Gill

Mastering English Literature will help readers both to enjoy English Literature and to be successful in 'O' levels, 'A' levels and other public exams. It is an introduction to the study of poetry, novels and drama which helps the reader in four ways – by providing ways of approaching literature, by giving examples and practice exercises, by offering hints on how to write about literature, and by the author's own evident enthusiasm for the subject. With extracts from more than 200 texts, this is an enjoyable account of how to get the maximum satisfaction out of reading, whether it be for formal examinations or simply for pleasure.

Work Out English Literature ('A' level)
S.H. Burton

This book familiarises 'A' level English Literature candidates with every kind of test which they are likely to encounter. Suggested answers are worked out step by step and accompanied by full author's commentary. The book helps students to clarify their aims and establish techniques and standards so that they can make appropriate responses to similar questions when the examination pressures are on. It opens up fresh ways of looking at the full range of set texts, authors and critical judgements and motivates students to know more of these matters.

Also from Macmillan

CASEBOOK SERIES

The Macmillan *Casebook* series brings together the best of modern criticism with a selection of early reviews and comments. Each Casebook charts the development of opinion on a play, poem, or novel, or on a literary genre, from its first appearance to the present day.

GENERAL THEMES

COMEDY: DEVELOPMENTS IN CRITICISM
D. J. Palmer

DRAMA CRITICISM: DEVELOPMENTS SINCE IBSEN
A. J. Hinchliffe

THE ENGLISH NOVEL: DEVELOPMENTS IN CRITICISM SINCE HENRY JAMES
Stephen Hazell

THE LANGUAGE OF LITERATURE
N. Page

THE PASTORAL MODE
Bryan Loughrey

THE ROMANTIC IMAGINATION
J. S. Hill

TRAGEDY: DEVELOPMENTS IN CRITICISM
R. P. Draper

POETRY

WILLIAM BLAKE: SONGS OF INNOCENCE AND EXPERIENCE
Margaret Bottrall

BROWNING: MEN AND WOMEN AND OTHER POEMS
J. R. Watson

BYRON: CHILDE HAROLD'S PILGRIMAGE AND DON JUAN
John Jump

CHAUCER: THE CANTERBURY TALES
J. J. Anderson

COLERIDGE: THE ANCIENT MARINER AND OTHER POEMS
A. R. Jones and W. Tydeman

DONNE: SONGS AND SONETS
Julian Lovelock

T. S. ELIOT: FOUR QUARTETS
Bernard Bergonzi

T. S. ELIOT: PRUFROCK, GERONTION, ASH WEDNESDAY AND OTHER POEMS
B. C. Southam

T. S. ELIOT: THE WASTELAND
C. B. Cox and A. J. Hinchliffe

ELIZABETHAN POETRY: LYRICAL AND NARRATIVE
Gerald Hammond

THOMAS HARDY: POEMS
J. Gibson and T. Johnson

GERALD MANLEY HOPKINS: POEMS
Margaret Bottrall

KEATS: ODES
G. S. Fraser

KEATS: THE NARRATIVE POEMS
J. S. Hill

MARVELL: POEMS
Arthur Pollard

THE METAPHYSICAL POETS
Gerald Hammond

MILTON: PARADISE LOST
A. E. Dyson and Julian Lovelock

POETRY OF THE FIRST WORLD
WAR
Dominic Hibberd

ALEXANDER POPE: THE RAPE OF
THE LOCK
John Dixon Hunt

SHELLEY: SHORTER POEMS &
LYRICS
Patrick Swinden

SPENSER: THE FAERIE QUEEN
Peter Bayley

TENNYSON: IN MEMORIAM
John Dixon Hunt

THIRTIES POETS: 'THE AUDEN
GROUP'
Ronald Carter

WORDSWORTH: LYRICAL
BALLADS
A. R. Jones and W. Tydeman

WORDSWORTH: THE PRELUDE
W. J. Harvey and R. Gravil

W. B. YEATS: POEMS 1919–1935
E. Cullingford

W. B. YEATS: LAST POEMS
Jon Stallworthy

THE NOVEL AND PROSE

JANE AUSTEN: EMMA
David Lodge

JANE AUSTEN: NORTHANGER
ABBEY AND PERSUASION
B. C. Southam

JANE AUSTEN: SENSE AND
SENSIBILITY, PRIDE AND
PREJUDICE AND MANSFIELD
PARK
B. C. Southam

CHARLOTTE BRONTË: JANE EYRE
AND VILLETTE
Miriam Allott

EMILY BRONTË: WUTHERING
HEIGHTS
Miriam Allott

BUNYAN: THE PILGRIM'S
PROGRESS
R. Sharrock

CONRAD: HEART OF DARKNESS,
NOSTROMO AND UNDER
WESTERN EYES
C. B. Cox

CONRAD: THE SECRET AGENT
Ian Watt

CHARLES DICKENS: BLEAK
HOUSE
A. E. Dyson

CHARLES DICKENS: DOMBEY
AND SON AND LITTLE DORRITT
Alan Shelston

CHARLES DICKENS: HARD TIMES,
GREAT EXPECTATIONS AND OUR
MUTUAL FRIEND
N. Page

GEORGE ELIOT: MIDDLEMARCH
Patrick Swinden

GEORGE ELIOT: THE MILL ON
THE FLOSS AND SILAS MARNER
R. P. Draper

HENRY FIELDING: TOM JONES
Neil Compton

E. M. FORSTER: A PASSAGE TO
INDIA
Malcolm Bradbury

HARDY: THE TRAGIC NOVELS
R. P. Draper

HENRY JAMES: WASHINGTON
SQUARE AND THE PORTRAIT OF
A LADY
Alan Shelston

JAMES JOYCE: DUBLINERS AND A
PORTRAIT OF THE ARTIST AS A
YOUNG MAN
Morris Beja

D. H. LAWRENCE: THE RAINBOW
AND WOMEN IN LOVE
Colin Clarke

D. H. LAWRENCE: SONS AND
LOVERS
Gamini Salgado

SWIFT: GULLIVER'S TRAVELS
Richard Gravil

THACKERAY: VANITY FAIR
Arthur Pollard

TROLLOPE: THE BARSETSHIRE
NOVELS
T. Bareham

VIRGINIA WOOLF: TO THE
LIGHTHOUSE
Morris Beja

DRAMA

CONGREVE: COMEDIES
Patrick Lyons

T. S. ELIOT: PLAYS
Arnold P. Hinchliffe

JONSON: EVERY MAN IN HIS
HUMOUR AND THE ALCHEMIST
R. V. Holdsworth

JONSON: VOLPONE
J. A. Barish

MARLOWE: DR FAUSTUS
John Jump

MARLOWE: TAMBURLAINE,
EDWARD II AND THE JEW OF
MALTA
John Russell Brown

MEDIEVAL ENGLISH DRAMA
Peter Happé

O'CASEY: JUNO AND THE
PAYCOCK, THE PLOUGH AND THE
STARS AND THE SHADOW OF A
GUNMAN
R. Ayling

JOHN OSBORNE: LOOK BACK IN
ANGER
John Russell Taylor

WEBSTER: THE WHITE DEVIL AND
THE DUCHESS OF MALFI
R. V. Holdsworth

WILDE: COMEDIES
W. Tydeman

SHAKESPEARE

SHAKESPEARE: ANTONY AND
CLEOPATRA
John Russell Brown

SHAKESPEARE: CORIOLANUS
B. A. Brockman

SHAKESPEARE: HAMLET
John Jump

SHAKESPEARE: HENRY IV PARTS
I AND II
G. K. Hunter

SHAKESPEARE: HENRY V
Michael Quinn

SHAKESPEARE: JULIUS CAESAR
Peter Ure

SHAKESPEARE: KING LEAR
Frank Kermode

SHAKESPEARE: MACBETH
John Wain

SHAKESPEARE: MEASURE FOR
MEASURE
G. K. Stead

SHAKESPEARE: THE MERCHANT
OF VENICE
John Wilders

SHAKESPEARE: A MIDSUMMER
NIGHT'S DREAM
A. W. Price

SHAKESPEARE: MUCH ADO
ABOUT NOTHING AND AS YOU
LIKE IT
John Russell Brown

SHAKESPEARE: OTHELLO
John Wain

SHAKESPEARE: RICHARD II
N. Brooke

SHAKESPEARE: THE SONNETS
Peter Jones

SHAKESPEARE: THE TEMPEST
D. J. Palmer

SHAKESPEARE: TROILUS AND
CRESSIDA
Priscilla Martin

SHAKESPEARE: TWELFTH NIGHT
D. J. Palmer

SHAKESPEARE: THE WINTER'S
TALE
Kenneth Muir

MACMILLAN SHAKESPEARE VIDEO WORKSHOPS

DAVID WHITWORTH

Three unique book and video packages, each examining a particular aspect of Shakespeare's work; tragedy, comedy and the Roman plays. Designed for all students of Shakespeare, each package assumes no previous knowledge of the plays and can serve as a useful introduction to Shakespeare for 'O' and 'A' level candidates as well as for students at colleges and institutes of further, higher and adult education.

The material is based on the New Shakespeare Company Workshops at the Roundhouse, adapted and extended for television. By combining the resources of television and a small theatre company, this exploration of Shakespeare's plays offers insights into varied interpretations, presentation, styles of acting as well as useful background information.

While being no substitute for seeing the whole plays in performance, it is envisaged that these video cassettes will impart something of the original excitement of the theatrical experience, and serve as a welcome complement to textual analysis leading to an enriched and broader view of the plays.

Each package consists of:

* the Macmillan Shakespeare editions of the plays concerned;

* a video cassette available in VHS or Beta;

* a leaflet of teacher's notes.

THE TORTURED MIND
looks at the four tragedies Hamlet, Othello, Macbeth and King Lear.

THE COMIC SPIRIT
examines the comedies Much Ado About Nothing, Twelfth Night, A Midsummer Night's Dream, and As You Like It.

THE ROMAN PLAYS
Features Julius Caesar, Antony and Cleopatra and Coriolanus